"The great Holocaust writer and survivor Elie Wiesel says that we are most universal when we are most particular. Michelle Warren takes us through her individual and particular journey in a way that powerfully reveals the core of the call to all of us, wherever we come from, to love mercy and do justice. A wonderful book for young Christians—and for all Christians who have begun to authentically wrestle with the demands of whole-gospel discipleship. Wise, funny, and well written. Read it!"

Alexia Salvatierra, coauthor of *Faith-Rooted Organizing*

"Michelle is one of our country's top organizers. She has a heart for people, a gift for organizing, and a commitment to marginalized communities. She is a voice we should be listening to today. I highly recommend her book to anyone who is interested in organizing and has a concern for people."

Leroy Barber, director, The Voices Project, board chair, Missio Alliance

"Michelle Warren is a faithful witness to the power of proximity. She writes like she lives—with great passion and purpose—and shows us the path to justice by sharing her own story with vulnerability and insight. *The Power of Proximity* urges us to overcome our fears and courageously cross the deep dividing lines within our society. We are challenged not only to get close to those who are hurting on the Jericho road, but to transform the whole road!"

Shawn Casselberry, executive director, Mission Year

"Michelle Warren is a genuine and credible expert on this topic. She and her family have personally lived out the value of proximity, and her work with everyone from neighborhood stakeholders to senior politicians has demonstrated that there really is untapped power here. I encourage you to allow Michelle to guide you on a journey into a new perspective on the intersection of faith and social engagement."

Daniel Hill, senior pastor, River City Community Church, author of *White Awake*

"Michelle Warren is a remarkable woman who, along with her husband and family, has lived among the poor for over two decades. They have learned so much from the people around them. Michelle weaves her story in touching and heartfelt ways that teach us all about the importance of proximity. I highly recommend *The Power of Proximity*."

Wayne "Coach" Gordon, pastor, Lawndale Community Church, president emeritus, Christian Community Development Association

"In the spirit of John Perkins's call to 'relocation' in the 1980s, Michelle Warren's *The Power of Proximity* calls a new generation to defy the moving sidewalk that pushes us to seek out and settle down in communities of comfort. Instead she says, 'Lean in.' Michelle's life and words declare that the renewing of our minds requi~   'oca- tion of our bodies into the epic day-to-day struggles ~f   to forgotten corners of our cities and towns. ~~   ty to heal and transform our world."

Lisa Sharon Harper, speaker, activist, auth~

"As a person of color who has long lived in the 'hood like Michelle Warren, I was eager to read how she deals with issues such as racial privilege, discouragement over our political system, and the plight of those without proper papers. . . . *The Power of Proximity* is a clear reminder to me of how solidarity with the poor is a way to God's heart."

Russell Jeung, professor, San Francisco State University, author of *At Home in Exile*

"We cannot effectively love our neighbors as ourselves, as Jesus commands us, unless we're in close proximity to them; we will never be good Samaritans if we avoid the Jericho road altogether. My friend Michelle Warren, who with her family has lived in close proximity to poor and vulnerable people for decades, offers this important challenge as to why awareness of injustice is not enough."

Matthew Soerens, US director of church mobilization, World Relief

"In an age of hashtag awareness and digital outrage, Michelle Warren invites us to embrace the power of the incarnation, to let our love for others and our passion for justice take on flesh and 'move into the neighborhood.' This is not a book, a collection of stories, or a set of principles; this is a life lived in self-giving love."

Glenn Packiam, lead pastor, New Life Downtown

"With the guiding voice of a mentor, Michelle instills in the reader the necessity of the intrusively life-altering work of proximity. Because injustice is not merely a case study, ongoing proximity is necessary to move toward justice. This book is a practical introduction for a young adult, especially a young adult from a community of privilege, who is seeking inspiration for shaping a lifestyle that reflects a just God."

Diana Collymore, assistant director of missions, InterVarsity Christian Fellowship/USA

"As Michelle Warren eloquently explores, there is simply no substitute for relationships. None. When we make relationships our priority, the transformative power of God is unleashed as we listen to and learn from those who are different from us. That's why I'm so grateful for this timely book. It's an excellent guide, grounded in a lifetime of experience, and it provides an alternative story to our polarized and fragmented culture."

Tim Soerens, cofounding director of The Parish Collective, coauthor of *The New Parish*

"I wholeheartedly affirm Michelle Warren's powerful storytelling about the personal transformation experienced when one makes the decision to live among precious people experiencing poverty."

Andy Bales, CEO, Union Rescue Mission of Los Angeles

"With disarming candor, Michelle Warren gently guides us to a pursuit of Jesus that unmasks our consensual hallucinations of ourselves heroically in charge, saving the world on our terms, or sated with stuff, status, security, and success. At the same time, with insight and vigor she chronicles a rich life of proximity with people in need and reminds us that in a world torn by trauma, there is nothing 'natural' in being neutral."

John Hayes, founder and general director, InnerCHANGE

The

POWER

of

PROXIMITY

Moving Beyond Awareness to Action

MICHELLE FERRIGNO WARREN

Foreword by **NOEL CASTELLANOS**

IVP Books

An imprint of InterVarsity Press
Downers Grove, Illinois

InterVarsity Press
P.O. Box 1400, Downers Grove, IL 60515-1426
ivpress.com
email@ivpress.com

*InterVarsity Press® is the book-publishing division of InterVarsity Christian Fellowship/USA®, a
movement of students and faculty active on campus at hundreds of universities, colleges, and schools
of nursing in the United States of America, and a member movement of the International Fellowship
of Evangelical Students. For information about local and regional activities, visit intervarsity.org.*

*All Scripture quotations, unless otherwise indicated, are taken from THE HOLY BIBLE,
NEW INTERNATIONAL VERSION®, NIV® Copyright © 1973, 1978, 1984, 2011 by Biblica, Inc.™
Used by permission. All rights reserved worldwide.*

*While any stories in this book are true, some names and identifying information may have been
changed to protect the privacy of individuals.*

Cover design: Faceout Studio
Interior design: Daniel van Loon

ISBN 978-0-8308-4390-9 (print)
ISBN 978-0-8308-8926-6 (digital)

Printed in the United States of America ♾

Library of Congress Cataloging-in-Publication Data

Names: Warren, Michelle Ferrigno, 1971- author.
*Title: The power of proximity : moving beyond awareness to action / Michelle
    Ferrigno Warren ; foreword by Noel Castellanos.*
*Description: Downers Grove : InterVarsity Press, 2017. | Includes
    bibliographical references.*
*Identifiers: LCCN 2017010366 (print) | LCCN 2017016957 (ebook) | ISBN
    9780830889266 (eBook) | ISBN 9780830843909 (pbk. : alk. paper)*
*Subjects: LCSH: Christianity and geography. | Church work with the poor. |
    Christian life.*
*Classification: LCC BR115.G45 (ebook) | LCC BR115.G45 W37 2017 (print) | DDC
    261.8/325--dc23*
LC record available at https://lccn.loc.gov/2017010366

| **P** | 21 | 20 | 19 | 18 | 17 | 16 | 15 | 14 | 13 | 12 | 11 | 10 | 9 | 8 | 7 | 6 | 5 | 4 | 3 | 2 | 1 |
| **Y** | 34 | 33 | 32 | 31 | 30 | 29 | 28 | 27 | 26 | 25 | 24 | 23 | 22 | 21 | 20 | 19 | 18 | 17 | | | |

To David—your passion and commitment

to living in proximity with the poor inspires my own.

CONTENTS

FOREWORD

Noel Castellanos

On a recent sabbatical, I had the privilege of completing a thousand-year-old religious pilgrimage in northern Spain known as El Camino de Santiago. The Camino was popularized more recently in a movie called *The Way* that introduces this five-hundred-mile trek with all of its challenges and adventures, although it did not do an adequate job of depicting the horrendous blisters that are the price everyone who walks this journey must endure.

I learned many lessons as I walked the Camino with my son Stefan and my daughter, Anna. Among them is the power of proximity and its relation to loving God and loving our neighbor. The Bible is filled with imagery about the Camino or the way. Jesus calls himself the Way, and makes a bold statement: "I am the way, the truth and the life, and no one comes to the Father except through me." In other words, no one can become who God has created them to be or experience what life was intended to be without being in close proximity to God. If we are honest, most of us would affirm what Jesus said. The way that leads to destruction is wide, and many people end up on that road. The way that leads to a life of love, compassion, and justice is narrow—especially for the poor.

The wide road is so tempting because it is so much easier to take than the narrow road. On the wide road, we have so much room to roam, living for ourselves and not worrying about the needs of others. We can insulate ourselves from the pain, inequity, and injustices all around us, and never come in close contact or proximity to the harsh realities of the majority of men, women, and children on our planet who live in extreme poverty. Astonishingly, many of these individuals created in the image of God live in our own nation, but depending on where we live and our background we can live our entire lives without knowing anyone who is poor or from a different race. Lack of proximity allows us the luxury of driving around the hurting without having to engage. The result is devastation, as the illusions of wealth, power, and freedom to live as we desire leave us alienated from God and from others, and ultimately leave us spiritually bankrupt.

The narrow road is less populated, but because it is narrow, it requires that we walk with others in tight quarters. Like riding in urban subways around the world, we are pressed together on our journey. There is no way to escape listening to the stories of not being able to pay this month's rent, or of having a loved one locked up in prison, or being deported by immigration officers. But in the midst of this chaos, we discover that we have one thing in common with every other human being—a deep longing for authentic love, redemption, hope and to be intimately connected with our creator. On the narrow road, the way of Jesus, we discover that in our common brokenness, we can experience new life, purpose, and community.

As I write this, I think about my daughter, Anna, who is about to graduate from St. Louis University's campus in Madrid, Spain, and who has a deep passion for the vulnerable and for justice. I can't wait for Anna to read Michelle's book because it will inspire her to continue running toward a life of ministry on the narrow road alongside the vulnerable—not to fix their problems as the "Great Brown Latina Hope" (although she is amazing), but to experience and recognize the power that living in close proximity to the poor has had on her life. Anna has lived that reality having been raised in our Mexican barrio on the west side of Chicago. And there are millions of young men and women just like Anna who need to know that by being willing to stay or enter into the pain of the vulnerable in our world, they can choose the way of Jesus, who became a Galilean Jew in an obscure Palestinian village and offered his life instead of hate to bring redemption to friend and foe alike, and to proclaim the good news that God became proximate in our world to demonstrate his love for all, especially for the vulnerable.

I am so grateful for Michelle and to her family for being willing to press in to a life of living in close proximity with their neighbors in Dallas and Denver all of these years. I'm grateful that we have an opportunity to work together through CCDA to address that need for Christians to engage in loving and serving alongside of the poor in our world, and I'm grateful that Michelle has shared her struggles, her convictions, and her wisdom in *The Power of Proximity*. My prayer to God is that he will use this book to help us overcome our own fears and insecurities—to express our faith in Jesus Christ by walking in close proximity to the poor as an expression of our love for him.

INTRODUCTION

*I*f you wake up in the morning and the system works for you, you think it's a good and just system. You frame the way you see the world through this lens. Your lens, shaped by your personal and collective experiences, helps craft a narrative that determines the way you move forward in the world.

I have had the privilege to wake up for many years looking through lenses framed by two different communities. Both are filled with people who love God and want to love each other well. Both long for unity, flourishing, and love. Both are rich in assets, designed to do something with what they know and what they have.

More than twenty years ago I chose to leave the community in which I was born and live in close proximity to the poor as an expression of justice. I don't think I realized then what I was doing. I just thought living alongside those with whom I worked and worshiped was better than driving in a few times a week to get my "job" done. Over time I have grown to understand my life's choices better. I wanted ours to be a shared way of life.

This idea of becoming proximate to the poor was not unique to my husband and me. John Perkins, a pastor from Jackson,

Mississippi, along with an amazing group of radical Christians, had been doing it for more than a decade before us. Dr. Perkins called living in proximity to the poor "relocation." This philosophy was shared by a number of Christians who not only served communities by relocating but lived out an additional seven principles that today we know as Christian community development (CCD).

The amazing thing is that it wasn't until six years after my husband, David, and I began to talk and then live our life alongside the poor that we learned of John Perkins, the CCD principles, and the association of people who practiced those principles. It turns out that proximity to the poor was not a philosophy; it was a movement of the Spirit, who continues to reconcile the world to himself and people to one another. My story is simply one that confirms his transformational work in the hearts of those who follow him—a movement that continues today.

The recent surge of millennials engaging in justice work around the globe is outstanding. While traveling around the country, talking to and meeting with young people about injustice and the response of the church, I hear a similar question over and over again: "What can I do to engage injustice and make real, lasting change?" These young people sincerely want to make an impact on the brokenness they see in the world around them.

The first few times I was asked how to engage injustice and make a difference, I would talk about what I had studied and how I had landed where I am today. But the more I heard these young people's questions, the more I realized they were ready to bring about change in the world now. They were not naive to pain and injustice like I had been years ago when I was considering church work among the urban poor. These vibrant young people were aware of the world's problems at a deep level. They were ready to take their awareness—learned in school, from social media, on short-term mission trips, and through international travel—to a more substantive level. They were serious about change and wanted to know how to pivot to their next move so they could do the most good.

I also realized that it wasn't just a few people who were thinking about these things. Requests to connect, to talk about the future, became a constant stream. Young people consistently asked, "What should I be studying? What internships should I line up? I want to advocate for justice as a Christian. I feel so passionate about __. What should be my next steps? How do I do what you're doing?"

What good news to the hurting world and to the church! Young people are ready to take part in the solutions to the problems that divide our country, our globe. Young people are ready to use their abilities to aid a dying world. This is outstanding! How exciting to know that God is raising up his people to meet the challenges of the future.

This book is an attempt to answer the questions I've heard more broadly than is possible in those one-on-one coffee meetings or walks I've taken this past decade with so many young adults. Of course age does not have to limit your engagement of injustice, nor should it. This book is written to the church too! Yet if you are anything like these young people I've met, I know you also want to do something with all the injustice you've learned about. You want to know what to do next. And my advice to you is the same as it has been to them. The most profound move you can make to address pain and injustice is to become proximate to it.

Proximity to anything gives you a front-row seat to what's happening. This is why tickets near the front of a sports stadium or concert venue are so expensive and valuable. You have the best view from the front and the experience is far more personal. Up close there is little debate about what's actually happening in front of you.

And you know what? Becoming proximate to the poor, those impacted most by injustice, is the most radical, transformative thing you can do to affect it. Proximity to the poor is powerful.

Not everyone has a front-row seat. The front row is a privilege, an opportunity to see what's really going on and to allow those factors to penetrate your heart and mind, bringing you to a place where you can participate in the transformation. People in the back can benefit from your perspective because they aren't there.

Learning about pain and injustice from a book or a short experience may tug at the strings of your heart, but it offers a very limited view. Certainly that faraway view can fan the flames of God's heart for justice embedded in yours and give you a vision of yourself helping to alleviate it. Studying theology, sociology, anthropology, or policy is also a great way to build your foundation as a person so you can better interact with the issues. But these actions are still limited. They keep you on the back of the bus away from the action.

In contrast, proximity to injustice transforms your view of the bigger world and the people moving about in it. Most importantly, it transforms you in all the ways that are necessary to help you take part in God's process of redeeming and rebuilding what is broken.

My proximity to the poor radically changed my perspective. This book is laced with stories of things I learned along my journey, but it is also filled with principles I gleaned to help others move forward on a path of impacting injustice in effective and sustaining ways. A proximity journey is very personal because personal starting points are so diverse, but the transformative work of proximity enables us to move forward with integrity together.

I love reading books about transformation, especially the transformation that happens in communities and inspiring stories of the poor moving their lives forward as a result of God's Spirit. These are good, important books in the work of engaging with injustice, but that is not the purpose of this book. This book is about personal transformation. It is designed to speak of the power of proximity, not simply tell stories of my proximate life. We need to understand injustice at its core so we can move toward its alleviation. I believe proximity is key, and this book is an attempt to spell out why a life lived in a community is so important in moving toward justice.

That said, my tendency is to want to tell you all those amazing stories of transformation among the people who worked so hard to allow God to bring them to a restored place. These are happy and uplifting stories. So you will hear some of them.

I am grateful for each day I have observed, learned, grown, laughed, cried, celebrated, and mourned in my proximity to the poor community. God's call to live in such a radical way was one of his greatest, most generous gifts to me. I have laughed louder and cried harder than I even knew was possible. As I look back on the past twenty-plus years, I find myself tremendously grateful for him and his plan. I would not ever have dreamed up such a beautiful, transformational story. He is a great author and finisher.

Still, I have chosen to leave out many of the names of people whose lives I have shared so the focus can be on individual transformation of people who live in proximity to the poor and not on the poor themselves who have taught me so much.

It is from this privileged seat, this place of proximity to staggering pain, injustice, and brokenness, that I invite you to join me. Journey with me, not only with a little of my story and transformed perspective, but also with my thoughts on how I believe the church should more deeply engage this justice narrative moving from awareness to action. Let's lean in, with eyes wide open, and learn to embrace the power of proximity.

Part One

PROXIMITY TRANSFORMS US

Chapter One

BECOMING PROXIMATE

My proximate journey began when my husband, David, and
I were dating. We started talking about our dreams for
the future, and while we had our separate dreams, we began to
formulate thoughts around what we shared. We were both excited,
since it quickly became clear that we would be working in some
type of ministry.

The more we talked, the more we knew we were going to be working
in poor urban communities. Those early conversations, laced with an-
ticipation and dreams, revolved around the question of where we would
live. My then-fiancé thought we needed to live in the same at-risk
community as those who attended our church so we could share the
joys and struggles of life with them, loving our neighbors as ourselves.
I wasn't as convinced and certainly not excited about the prospect.

I grew up in predominantly white suburban communities, attended private Christian schools, and was heavily involved in

those communities. To say I was inexperienced and unaware was the understatement of the century. David, who had grown up in small, rural midwestern towns, was in a similar situation. We both shared strong stereotypes about the urban poor that we would have to overcome.

Stereotypes are powerful, and mine were no different. One I picked up along the way was that living close to the poor was dangerous and unwise. I had never even considered moving out of a "safe" community where I would be surrounded by "good, law-abiding" people with excellent schools, strong property values, and so on. Moving into a low-income neighborhood was a hard choice for me and everyone else in my world. At times it felt more like a social experiment than a lifestyle to attain.

At the time I did not think living in proximity to the poor was an important aspect of doing ministry alongside them. Living in the inner city back in the early nineties seemed not only like throwing my own life away but offering up our yet-to-be-born children's lives and opportunities as well.

While a life of proximity to the poor was one of those premarital nonnegotiables I really had to evaluate, I believed God was moving and I wanted to join his plans for our life. I chose to trust that God didn't want to ruin my life or future. I also had no intention of living my life as a martyr. I was just going to have to look at life through a new lens.

This new lens did not develop overnight but started with a decision in my heart that grew with what I saw and experienced. I specifically asked God to give me new eyes to see the poor with compassion and not fear. I asked him to give me a hopeful outlook for a long life in a new place.

My first transformation was to begin to see neighbors and not neighborhoods. Up until our decision to become proximate to the poor, I had always thought I would "choose" where I lived. I would pick the best neighborhood I could afford. Who knows—I might even get a greenbelt or two and a community pool. I had not been thinking about people, just myself and my future family's interests. Proximity to the poor was a radically different way of thinking. We were choosing to live alongside the poor and learn how to be good neighbors.

Becoming a Good Neighbor

While Jesus was on earth, a religious expert asked him an easy yet foundational question. "What must somebody do to inherit eternal life?" Instead of answering, Jesus replied with another question: "What is written in the Law? How do you read it?" The expert said, "Love the Lord your God with all your heart, soul, mind, and strength and your neighbor as yourself." Jesus affirmed him: "You answered correctly."

The expert, wanting to justify himself in this exchange, asked a follow-up question: "Who is my neighbor?" This led to one of Jesus' most familiar parables—the story of the Good Samaritan.

The story is about four people who were on a journey along the Jericho road. This road was dangerous and to be avoided if at all possible. If you traveled it, you did not want to be alone. In the story, one traveler was attacked by thieves and left on the side of the road beaten and half-dead. The three other travelers saw him along their way. One was a priest and another a Levite who hurriedly walked past the man, disregarding his condition. The third traveler, a Samaritan, took time to stop, help the wounded man, and take him to physical safety, paying for him to be physically restored. Thus he embodied the very definition of a good neighbor.

We Christians know the lesson of the parable is to make sure we aren't like the Levite or the priest but that we choose to be good neighbors like the Samaritan. We have to be willing to stop, get off our agenda, and help a person along their journey, even if that journey involves being beaten up and left for dead.

Throughout our world, all kinds of half-dead beaten-up people are lying on the side of the road in need of a Good Samaritan willing to help them find healing and safety. If we look at statistics, we find that many are women and children. Many come from families that have been in poverty for generations. In this day and age, the luxury of being ignorant to this global reality is over. News, pictures, and videos are ever-present, making us aware of others' pain and begging for a response. How can we begin to piece together solutions, motivated by love, that can begin to repair the brokenness and the injustices we see on today's Jericho roads?

As Christians we must not simply settle for awareness of the broken people on roads far away. Instead, we as the church must move together toward a proximate, informed response that moves toward the alleviation of injustice.

I believe the church, knowing the parable of the Good Samaritan and what a "good" neighbor is supposed to do, wants to respond. I believe Christians can choose to walk the Jericho road and become proximate to the half-dead beaten-up people lying along it. Knowing about pain and injustice from a distance is simply not enough to do anything of substance.

Why Awareness Isn't Enough

Proximity changes our perspective and broadens our vision. As American Christians within the pragmatic evangelical paradigm, we recognize all too well that our vision is limited, so we spend money, time, and resources to shape and expand our lens.

We invest in Christian discipleship and education materials so we can be grounded in the truth of the Bible. We collect money and give it to leaders who go all over the world and into our own backyards to help people who don't have as much. We even work to develop good, strong outreach ministries to give people on our staffs, in our youth groups, and even in our adult congregations the chance to see and learn from others who are less fortunate so we can more deeply understand the world in which we live.

These are all good things. As someone who personally needed an expanded lens, I think participation in vision-broadening experiences is important. Of course, we try not to treat the broken or poor of society as zoo animals to be viewed in awe but instead work to do little acts of kindness and compassion that help bring us to a different place of understanding. As Christians we want to be aware of what we do not know so we can understand and embrace our shared humanity with a suffering world. These awareness experiences strike the chords of our heart in such a way that we feel, we hurt, we try to understand—and sometimes, we try to help.

Awareness also keeps us from getting stuck in our rut of privilege and gives us a cause around which we can redirect our self-absorbed lives for a moment. It gives us some meaning and helps us put our theology into ministry practice. When we put ministry into practice it helps us catch God's mission to rescue the world.

Conferences, books, video clips, mission trips, and so on are all helpful ways to stay relevant and remain aware. Talk of justice in our Christian circles is a good start. It shows that we are hungry for something more than privileged ignorance. At this point in church history we can become deeply aware of the hurts and pains of our world. However, for Christ-followers, this is not enough.

Awareness of injustice is never enough. The true justice Christians say they seek is justice that sits as the foundation of God's throne and demands that we move beyond learning about injustice.

Injustice is not something to be aware of, it is something to engage, because to know is to do.

The word *justice* has become so overused and misunderstood that its deep, transformational work has become codified and is beginning to lose its value. Justice, radical in nature, is becoming routine. It has been watered down in such a way that we think we are drinking deeply, but eventually we come to realize that it's not enough. To simply be aware of injustice has limited lasting value.

Awareness is not enough to fix a broken system. It is not enough to affect the status quo. It is not enough to keep us or anyone else engaged for the long haul. It does not make enough of an impact on our collective lens, and, more tragically, it does not transform our lens in a way that will bring about true liberation for those trapped in broken systems.

Proximity does all of these things. Proximity gets us so close to the pain of an issue that it radically changes our perspective and demands a deeper response. The longer we stay proximate, the more our perspective is shaped and the more we respond to what needs to be changed. Proximity is transformational. It unearths the rules of our social construct and levels the playing field enough that we are able to journey with those impacted by injustice in deeply shared ways.

Unsettling Reality

When my husband and I moved into our first community in Dallas, Texas, we were the only white and married people in our apartment building. Having grown up next door to an African American family during my childhood, our situation didn't initially feel un-usual. But intersecting with poverty and single moms and their kids was entirely new. Our apartment building was filled with stereotypical low-income families. Men in and out, women and children living life, loud music playing, barbecues with way too much lighter fluid, lots of noise and roaches.

Proximate living was the most powerful way for me to learn to practice valuing people. Living life together reveals one another's truths.

In addition to living as a dominant culture minority in our community, I taught middle school math. Teaching gave me a front-row view to my new life, and it took all of about a second to know I knew nothing and to keep moving forward. With each new shocking reality, I would push through by reciting an internal mantra. I would tell myself, "You have lived a very sheltered life. Don't be shocked at anything." I'm not sure if this was a healthy coping mechanism, but it was what I used to get me through those early and *very* shocking first few years in my community.

Proximity to the poor does not just reveal what we don't know; it teaches us things no article, conference, class, or book can convey. We cannot understand problems from a distance. We cannot respect people if we don't know them or see them and their contributions closely. They are our teachers; we are their students. We must recognize and assume a posture of listening and learning in order to allow them to shape our lens.

Somewhere in humanity's history we began to believe that a person's financial worth is what makes them valuable and not their God-given position in the world. The dignity and worth of human beings is established in Genesis 1 with the *imago Dei*, and as Christians we should take that as our starting point when we look at people. During creation the Trinity actively spoke the world into existence, concluding with the formation of humanity. Here we see that humanity was not only created in God's image—the *imago Dei*—but also created with purpose:

Then God said, "Let us make mankind in our image, in our likeness, so that they may rule over the fish in the sea and the birds in the sky, over the livestock and all the wild animals, and over all the creatures that move along the ground."

So God created mankind in his own image,
in the image of God he created them;
male and female he created them.

God blessed them and said to them, "Be fruitful and increase in number; fill the earth and subdue it. Rule over the fish in the sea and the birds in the sky and over every living creature that moves on the ground." (Genesis 1:26-28)

Humanity's dominion over the created order was established at the beginning of time before class and social orders became the status quo. For those of us who were born into comfort and opportunity rather than poverty and injustice, we need to intentionally undo the results of sin that says certain people—especially those who are poor—have less to contribute. In proximity to the poor, we have the opportunity to become students of all they have to offer and we must position ourselves as ready to learn even as we bring what we have to share.

For me, teaching in at-risk schools provided an up-front, close, and personal picture into the painful and unstable life of the poor. As hard as it was to watch, I needed to learn and understand.

Every day I asked kids who lived in extraordinarily bad circumstances to come on time with a sharpened pencil, ready to formally study subjects that would not help them with their immediate survival and success. Students would ask to go to the nurse because they were having trouble with morning sickness. Students regularly switched schools because moms had new boyfriends, housing project vouchers expired, and other reasons, which kept the school community in a constant unsettled motion. My students were drug-running, sexually active, abuse-surviving, low-scoring, gang-savvy kiddos.

Schools in my community were trying to survive from one day to the next. The kids came from such difficult lives that the thought of actually learning something that could level the playing field with their contemporaries from my former world felt outrageous. Day after day, concept after concept, we worked our way through multiplication facts, the conversion of fractions to decimals. We were buying time until we made it to the annual test, which would label us a successful group of workers or not.

No one told me kids with disabilities or without English language skills were being mainstreamed into my class. No one told me much of anything, actually. It was a "Good luck—don't get killed or let anyone else kill each other!" kind of environment. In my ignorance and lack of guided instruction, I found myself always a step behind.

After teaching a few months I was told I needed to oversee before-school playground duty. So I walked out to where students got dropped off by the buses. I wasn't on the playground for more than ten minutes when I saw students rush off the bus and circle two kids who were having a standard, run-of-the-mill knife fight. I saw from a distance what was happening and ran inside to get help. I rushed through the lines where kids were getting their bags checked by metal detectors, yelling over a pack of kids to the assistant principal who was a few yards away. I was in a panic.

The assistant principal calmly took his walkie-talkie and shared what was happening. I ran back outside as fast as I could. I was trying to get over to the group when out of the corner of my eye I saw the head principal, his jacket billowing like a superhero cape, running down the hill to the fight. He was there in a flash and wrestled a kid to the ground. How he knew which one to take down so the fighting would stop I will never know. But just like that it was over. Kids left the circle, the two students went off to juvie, and we never saw them again. We all went back to business as usual. No one mentioned it. There was no counseling for students who had just witnessed the bloody scene or for me.

That pretty much sums up life among the urban poor. Alarming, shocking things happen all the time, and when the immediate danger is over, we go back to surviving one day at a time. The fragility of life became apparent to me early on, but so did its strength. My neighbors were tremendously resilient in the midst of constant challenges. They repeatedly demonstrated the ability to move forward despite their circumstances. This was not simple positivity. This was a decision to hope. I needed to not only see and share in the experience of their pain, lack of access, and needs—I needed to learn from them how to survive and gain the strength to remain planted in our community, committed to moving forward together.

My Choice, Their Reality

Becoming proximate to the poor reinforces our chosen life and their reality. The hard things I saw and experienced revealed not only my limited ability to make an impact but the reality of my mobility. It was ever before me as I entertained the idea of returning to my community of origin and escaping the pain I was experiencing. I could decide to move into a community and choose where to work, but this was not the case with my students and their families. This was the system they were born into; there was nothing temporary or trite about it. Life and death hung in the balance every day for them. My privilege and my chosen proximity remained apparent. This was sobering.

One morning in my first year of teaching, I arrived at school to find a group of teachers huddled together talking. Two students would not be coming back because they had gotten into a knife fight on the bus the afternoon before. The victim was a pregnant girl who was still in the hospital because of the injuries she had sustained. Apparently another student had stolen a pair of long-sheared scissors from a teacher's desk, brought it onto the bus, and stabbed the girl sitting ahead of her in the neck. The horrors of this kind of violence were par for the course. The news wasn't that it had happened but that it involved a teacher's scissors.

Standing there, I realized pretty quickly that the group was berating the idiot teacher who hadn't locked her door or kept track of her stuff when students were in her classroom. I felt that the accusations were being directed toward me. I was sick and scared. I was probably the teacher who had done this. How could I have been so stupid? One of our pregnant seventh-graders was in the hospital and I was probably to blame.

I quietly walked into my classroom and closed the door. With fear and shame I opened the top drawer to my desk to see if my classroom-issued scissors were there. They were. It hadn't been me. While I was temporarily relieved, I knew it easily could have been me. My decisions had life-and-death ramifications for the people around me. I was sobered by this realization.

This is not a social experiment; this is the very lives of other people. This is not about me; it is about them. I was young and inexperienced. I needed to keep pushing forward: "You have lived a sheltered life. Don't be surprised at anything." But my heart was breaking for what I was seeing.

Staying Rooted

Words cannot explain the culture shock I walked through during those early years. No one in my former life or even my young married Sunday school class at the white privileged church I attended knew what I was seeing daily and the concerns in my head and heart. At times I was afraid. I didn't know who to tell, so I told no one. I was not equipped with practical ways to engage this explicitly broken culture. I knew that if I began to share what I was seeing, I would be told to come home, and that was not a choice I wanted to make.

During those early months of teaching I began to have trouble sleeping for worry over which student would not be there the next day. Fridays were difficult because as I said goodbye I wondered who would return on Monday. The weekends were deadly. Going back to school to see who was still there was painful.

After several months, God had mercy on me, and each individual's problem began to be defined as one big problem all pointing to the broken system surrounding the poor. My mind relaxed and I began to live each day with a hopeful optimism about what would—or, better yet, would *not*—happen next. I can't explain it. It wasn't so much a peace as much as it was a cultural reorientation. I was staying planted and committed to my decision. A new lens was beginning to take shape.

Those years teaching in at-risk schools in Dallas shaped my lens and provided an opportunity to continue to learn and navigate my new world. My season as a teacher allowed me to learn firsthand about the brokenness of my community that laid a foundation for my future understanding of the poor on even deeper levels.

Living in poor communities reveals the differences between those who choose to live in proximity to the poor and those who *are* poor. While it may cause us to doubt our ability to do anything of substance, we need to keep our eyes wide open and be students of our communities. We need to learn not only about them but from them.

The up-front, personal perspective I continued to gain did not just humanize these issues for me but led me to engage in ways I could not have imagined those many years ago when David and I first decided to move into a neighborhood and endeavor to love our neighbors as ourselves.

A commitment to proximate living means striving to be a good neighbor, to be deeply engaged from a personal place, to be willing to remain rooted and learn from the people around us, to glean from their strength, to admit the sobering reality that ours is a chosen place in contrast to their pain. Being proximate is necessary to engage brokenness because it transforms our lens. We cannot learn from a distance. We need a deeper, more informed perspective into ourselves, our communities, and the restoration we all seek.

Chapter Two

DEEPER AND HIGHER

*I*n addition to bringing my hopes and dreams for the future along with everything we owned in a small U-Haul trailer to Dallas, I brought my love for God and his people and a desire to see his work move forward in our broken world. Because I was being confronted daily with more and more challenging and unfamiliar situations, my view of God, his Son Jesus, and the work of the Holy Spirit was forced to grow in depth and richness.

It's hard to believe that something as foundational and timeless as theology would be so greatly impacted by location. But where we live and invest our lives shapes the way we do everything, and our attitudes toward the Bible and God are no different.

My personal theology has always been rooted in the Bible and my view of God based on foundational principles that transcend history and culture. I believe the Bible is a relevant book for today and tomorrow no matter where a person lives. However, that doesn't mean the way I perceived its truth or read its stories did not change when I began to live alongside the poor.

When our lens is shaped by proximity to the poor, the way we view right and wrong begins to shift our social construct in subtle ways. A social construct is an idea or ideal formed in context. It grows out of societal ideals, so it can impart a sense of authority about the correct or incorrect way to act or believe. Social construct goes beyond social mores; it is based on our understanding of what is acceptable and right. As an educated, privileged white American my social construct was limited to that perspective, which is why proximity to the poor was so powerful—it forced my view to expand.

This expansion can present a challenge. Social construct can mask itself as truth in such a way that when you begin to alter or shift it, it feels "wrong." When we live in proximity to the poor and we are not poor, it's easy to think that our version of acceptability is more appropriate for our neighbors than their ways of thinking and doing. In my earlier years of proximity, this was a challenging reality. I had to learn that what I perceived as the "right way" had no moral bearing, and people did not have to be like me. They needed to live out their God-given potential the way God intended, not the way I thought was appropriate.

Deepening Justice

I thought I understood justice early in my spiritual journey. It's a familiar word, used throughout the Bible and common in both Christian and secular circles. Before I moved to my proximate place with the poor, I always viewed justice in terms of punishment. I knew God was a God of justice, but I often associated that with his wrath. Justice is something we value as a society, but I have learned that we all perceive it differently depending on where we sit. We seem to treat justice as relative.

The Hebrew word for "justice" is *mishpat,* and we see in Psalm 89:14 that it forms God's very throne: "Righteousness and justice are the foundation of your throne; love and faithfulness go before you." While the psalmist is giving us a metaphor, the takeaway is that justice is foundational to who God is. How can something that is the foundation of God's throne be relative? It cannot.

Theology does not change relative to experience. And God's justice is not relative. Experiences can help inform our theological lens and challenge us to expand it beyond our limited understanding, but God does not change.

Expanding my view of justice was not simply a theological exercise. It was the process of being challenged by what I was seeing and experiencing. This is why proximity is powerful. It transforms our perspective of what we believe to be good and right. We cannot judge from afar but instead are required to sift what we are learning through theology to "test and approve" what God's perfect will really is (Romans 12:2).

One Sunday when my husband, David, was preaching at a local church, he spoke on God's justice and on his jubilee. For the first time I heard the Hebrew word for justice—*mishpat.* Not being a theologian or having studied Hebrew, I was intrigued by David's explanation of how *mishpat* is not simply punishment but that it hangs in a balance, like a pendulum, freely swinging between opportunity and consequence to help a person move to their productive place. Justice was about the restoration of people, not solely about punishment of wrongdoing.

My eyes were opened that day. I began to see the work we were doing as far more than small acts of compassion or mercy and the creation of rules and structure to help people order their chaotic lives. I longed to be a part of people's restoration in new and active ways in addition to providing them with new opportunities. This new viewpoint helped me begin to see that I could do more than simply stop on the side of the Jericho road and pick my neighbors up. I could walk alongside them to a restored place.

In his book *Just Generosity*, Ron Sider examines the biblical foundation for justice, or *mishpat*. He explains that it includes both procedural justice, which many of us are familiar with, and economic fairness—the lack of which I once believed was the fault of the poor.

"Biblical justice has both an economic and legal focus," Sider writes. "The goal of justice is not only integrity in the legal system, it also includes the restoration of the community as a place where all live together in wholeness." He goes on to explain that "restoration to community is central to justice." Because justice moves between opportunity and consequences to actions of restoration, we learn that "justice demands both fair courts and fair economic structures. It includes both freedom rights and benefit rights. Precisely because of its equal concern for wholeness for everyone, it pays special attention to the needs of the weak and marginalized."

In essence, God's justice recognizes that the poor need special attention. The poor need to be restored to their productive place so that the community can move forward together. If they are unable to move forward, we as agents of God's justice are not doing what we are called to do.

Social Construct

While an expanded, proximate-to-the-poor lens forces a deepening of our theology, it also causes us to elevate our social construct to a more prominent place in our thinking. I am not speaking here of cultural sensitivity. Of course, cultural sensitivity is crucial anytime we move into a new environment. Whether we encounter subtle or overt differences, it's important to recognize them and adapt. But social construct shaped by deepening theology is more foundational than cultural differences.

I remember when I was new to living with the urban poor in my apartment in Dallas. I had always been a barefoot kind of person. It was very hot in Dallas and unless I was headed somewhere special, I did not wear shoes. I had never given it a second thought— that was simply how I felt most comfortable. Because apartment living with hospitality in mind means open doors and a lot of stairway chatter, it was evident to my neighbors that I did not often wear shoes. My neighbors on the other hand never went barefoot.

One day I walked into my neighbor's apartment and she gave me a brand-new pair of slippers. I had never owned slippers as an adult. No one in my world ever wore them except maybe on Christmas morning with a robe. In my culture slippers were optional, unnecessary footwear that were more about being "cozy" than anything else. This was not the case in my new neighborhood. Wearing something on your feet was a must. I was too young and naive to even realize this was a cultural difference I should adjust to.

All these years later I can still see my neighbor casually handing me those soft white slippers, assuring me she had plenty and to take them. The gift felt warm and inviting. But the greater kindness was that she gently helped me understand how someone was supposed to go about in her community. I wore those slippers for years, always remembering my neighbor's thoughtfulness and my newfound awareness of cultural norms. Once you adjust to them, everyone becomes a bit more comfortable.

But beginning to deconstruct our social construct is a more challenging process. Wrestling in our heart with change can feel exciting at times, but for the most part it's lonely. There is no way to explain everything that takes place when we lean into proximity, but as we work to understand the world around us, we can be open to listening, learning, and expanding our ideology.

Social construct is not as foundational as theology, but it does have a way of tripping us up and limiting our ability to see people. The reason proximity to the poor is powerful is that it slowly erodes our view of ourselves and our way of life and then expands our view of the world. We are stronger when we realize how much we can learn from diversity. The hiccup happens when we share our ideals in a way that minimizes the experiences and perspectives of others.

One social construct I held in my early years was the idea that America was a Christian nation built on inherently good principles, and the problem with the poor was that they weren't practicing individual responsibility. They needed to pull it together, get a job, and be like the rest of society. Somewhere along the way in my growing up, this is the framework I obtained and from which I operated when I began living in proximity to the poor.

This was not the only social construct that shaped my perspective. Big issues around racism, money, politics, family, work, and education were constantly challenged in my new life, as were little ones such as homeownership, leisure time, how your front lawn looked, and how you maintained your car. My experience was not unique. Moving into proximity forces us to come to grips with how we see God and the world and how we think it should all move forward.

Our social constructs can even cause us to become tribalistic, keeping us from being molded by anyone else's thought lest we become corrupted by "the other side." I have seen tribalism subtly make its way into Christian communities, dividing the body into parts that don't communicate or respect one another. Years ago our attitude used to be something like "If I don't agree with you, I don't like you; I will avoid you." Now it's "If I don't agree with you, I hate you; don't come near me." This inability to allow someone else's ideas to impact us keeps us from understanding our differences and hinders the growth we can experience from a learning posture. As a result, we are unable to work together. We hang out with our tribe. We know best. We're fine the way we are.

The Dilemma

Growing up in my conservative Christian culture, you were either a Republican who believed in rugged individualism or you were wrong. My neighbors in proximity to the poor would say that if you care about people and their voice, you have to be a Democrat. What was I going to do? I was left having to experience this new life and think for myself—and I did both.

In the city, the sense of community is strong. Everyone feels responsible for the rearing of children and they act on it. People have varying levels of resources, and sharing is a way of life. Do you have some spare change? Can I borrow a cigarette? Will you give me a ride? Can I use your lawnmower?

Those with possessions were once in a place where they were without, so they don't hesitate to take their barely working car across town to drop you and your kids off after work because they know how long the bus takes. My formerly homeless friends would give change without reservation to those holding a sign asking for money because they had been there too. You know you can't do it by yourself, so you help when you can. What kind of people take care of only themselves?

Me.

Rugged individualism was a core value I had to overcome. You can borrow my lawnmower a few times, but eventually you need to get your own lawnmower—or don't have a lawn. Looking out for others and sharing what I had was not as easy as I would have thought. I had headed into the city to be generous, but day after day, request after request made me see my own selfishness. The life I came from where everyone was expected to take care of themselves was now radically different. I saw how individualistic my view of people was, and it made me wonder if my social construct of rugged individualism was biblical or humanmade.

As I continued to spend time in my new community of proximity, I also realized that the political affiliations and American idealism of my origins were not as eagerly embraced by my new neighbors. Unions were a way of life, police officers were feared, and social services were not looked on with disdain. Employers would set hours high enough to get what they wanted but low enough to deny their employees the health coverage they needed and desired. Access to opportunity and resources was limited. Services such as job training classes and temporary housing, while good and necessary, were barely scratching the surface of the brokenness in our community.

I began to see the complexities of the systems surrounding the poor: lack of education and access to jobs providing a livable wage, felonies disproportionately affecting people of color, families dealing with generations of abuse and addiction, insufficient access to health care, and high housing costs driving up our city's homeless were just a few factors. These were not statistics or news articles; they were the real lives of my friends and fellow churchgoers, and no one person had gotten themselves to this place alone.

One particular night I received a call just as night was becoming morning. It was from a friend in our church. Her granddaughter was threatening to kill herself. The police had been there a few hours before and left. Now things were so bad she didn't know what to do. Could I come?

I put on my clothes, got into my car, and drove over to her apartment. The wailing and rage coming from the granddaughter's room broke my heart. I sat with the girl on her bed and we cried together. After some time we all got in the car and drove to the children's hospital to have her admitted to the psych ward. When I walked in I handed the nurse her Medicaid card and breathed a silent prayer of thanks that medical bills were not something this little girl, with no father or mother to care for her, would have to worry about. Maybe government programs weren't so evil after all.

Countless experiences like this one were beginning to butt up against my social construct and challenge the depth to which I would choose to love my neighbor.

Loving Your Neighbor Justly

I'd like to focus this next section on mercy, justice, and loving your neighbor. I will be referring to the parable of the Good Samaritan to help explain these distinctions, as I believe the Jericho road is a metaphor for living in proximity to the poor and helps explain loving your neighbor with justice. Loving with justice includes individual, social, and systemic restoration.

Although the Jericho road in biblical times was a place everyone needed to travel at some point since it was the only road from Jerusalem to Jericho, walking the Jericho road in the twenty-first century is a choice, hence the "chosen proximity" of which I have been speaking. Let's compare the Jericho road to a modern highway.

Highway living is where things work. You might not have the most expensive car on the road, but it's a pretty comfortable ride. If something breaks, it gets fixed and you move on. This is life in the fast lane, or at least the faster lane.

The Jericho road is dangerous. Thieves wait to rob and steal from you there. This is the road people like me were taught to avoid lest we get beaten up and left in the ditch. It is weathered and used often. The sheer number of people traveling along it with all their clamor and ridiculous ways makes walking it pretty common, unless you are one of the privileged.

It's not hard to imagine a rocky path riddled with potholes, and while this road is not only for the low-income masses—remember that a Levite, a priest, and a Samaritan walked it too—it is a place to beware.

As I have walked this road over and over again I have met Levites, priests, Samaritans, thieves, and people beaten up on the side of the road. All the while I have thought of the twenty-first-century highway from which I came, yet I challenged myself to keep walking the broken road.

I set this stage because it's what we need to recognize about proximity. For the privileged, life alongside those on the Jericho road is a choice, which means that there are issues on the road with which we who are privileged cannot identify. Even so, it is important to get close enough for these issues to catch our attention and teach us how best to engage.

As Christians we know we're not supposed to be the Levite or the priest. We cannot be too busy on our way or too afraid or too inconvenienced to stop and help a beaten-up person rather than leave him to remain dying on the side of the road. We are compelled to love that person whether it feels natural or not.

But on the highway I was born to, people of faith didn't go down the Jericho road—ever! We didn't have to worry about being inconvenienced or too busy because it seemed reasonable to us to stay off that road so we didn't get hurt. How dumb someone would have to be to go down that road!

Oh, we might have visited the safest stretch in broad daylight with armed bodyguards on a youth group mission trip when we were teens. We went hoping to see a beaten-up and dying man on the side of the road, take a couple of selfies for the video montage, and maybe even help the beaten man to safety. But walking that road was *not* a way of life.

For those of us who did come to travel that road as a way of life, the ability to minister to the dying was transformative and lens-shifting. We saw clearly how dirty, smelly, and optionless the road was. We learned what we would always know afterward: this road stinks, and if at all possible, we have to help people get off or through it.

Individual Response and Restoration

After our time in Dallas, David and I moved to Denver and began to work at Open Door Fellowship, a small church in a poor area of the city's downtown. We started a transitional house whose purpose was to help homeless teen girls get off the street.

Girls who lived under bridges, on friends' couches, or hidden in alleys would come to our door asking for a place to stay and rest as they began to think about their path forward. Each girl came with her unique story; each was looking for safety and shelter. We greeted each one with a warm place to sleep, food to eat, and support. Responding to their immediate needs was an act of mercy and compassion.

After a girl had lived with us for a few days, regaining a small sense of stability, we would begin to talk about next steps. I remember one young woman who had left her family when she was fourteen. In an effort to conform to life on the streets she shaved her long hair into a Mohawk and dressed like a boy so she looked less like a victim. She wanted to move forward but did not know how to do that without support. We needed to think about what restoration looked like for her.

We started by contacting her parents so they knew she was alive and where she was living. Not being a foster care facility but a temporary haven, we tried to help restore the broken relationship with her family to see if they could all try again. This, along with getting her back into school and taking other steps toward restoration, was us moving from compassion toward justice.

When we respond to the immediate needs of the poor, we are choosing to be merciful. That is good, but that is not necessarily justice. Justice is not a response to a problem, mercy is. Justice looks beyond the problem to see how people ended up in that broken place and works to overcome barriers so they can be restored.

On the Jericho road we see mercy as well as a deep longing for restoration of the man who was beaten up and left for dead. The Good Samaritan helps the man get off the road in the moment, but then he stays overnight and even provides money to provide for the man's needs while he is away. We see in the text that he intends to return after a season to see how else he can support the victim's full restoration.

Helping individuals who have been beaten up resonates with our Christian social construct that says individual sanctification is the foundation and often the stopping point for the expression of Christian love. If we run into broken people, we help them individually. When we are broken, we either get help for ourselves or pray that it finds us. If we continue to personally help ourselves and those individuals we meet, we are loving our neighbor well. Helping neighbors is literal and is limited to individuals.

I refer to this as individual restoration. A person gets her individual life together with or without the help of another person, gets up, and moves forward.

Social Justice

Those of us who have chosen the Jericho road and continue to encounter its treachery recognize that certain conditions cause numerous travelers to be beaten up. We realize that beaten people should not be seen and helped only on an individual basis but that there are enormous societal issues that need addressing to help the hurting.

This is the reason we helped start a transitional house for homeless teen girls. We knew our community needed something to help address its homeless teen issue. In addition to homeless teenagers, our community struggles with addictions, affordable housing, childcare needs for working parents, job training skills, connections to employment, and many other social issues. Addressing the underlying issues in our society through development programs is what we call social justice ministry. The year after we began the transitional house for teenage girls, David started a church-based community development organization called Open Door Ministries. ODM continues to be the outreach and social justice ministry arm of Open Door Fellowship Church.

If we follow the journey on the Jericho road, social justice might look like setting up clinics to help those who get hurt along their journey or teaching classes on how to stay safe and unharmed as you walk the road. We may work to establish a community that walks together so people don't fall prey to thieves and robbers. Some have even created opportunities for others to get off the Jericho road and travel the highway for a faster, more efficient way.

All of this is good, albeit hard, social justice work. There is no substitute for this kind of up-close and personal journey. While we are on it, whether for a season or a lifetime, we are transformed over and over again. Those who have chosen to pour themselves out as a drink offering in service on this road are the kind of people who have had their perspective radically changed.

My family and I have lived daily on this road. We have chosen to invest our lives and futures in serving those who are hurt by society's ills. It was not out of a noble cause for the hurting or broken but out of simple obedience to the One who gave up everything to join our messy world.

In my earlier years of ministry, I thought that was the epitome of loving your neighbor. And had I not been born on another road, maybe I would have stayed in that thinking. But one day I realized I could not help enough people stay safe or get off the road if they wanted. Oh, sure, I could help a few here or there, but mental illness, poverty, and brokenness that I could never understand kept people stuck on that awful road.

That's when I realized that in addition to helping individuals we encounter and supporting social justice programs for those impacted by the road's harm, we also have got to fix the road.

Engaging Systemic Injustice

This brings us to engaging systemic injustice as an act of loving our neighbor. We live in the twenty-first century in the most resourced country in the world. We drive on highways and avoid the Jericho road or assume it cannot be changed. But the truth is that there should be no Jericho roads where the overprivileged don't have to walk and where the underprivileged cannot be safe or leave. We cannot pretend that insufficient, broken roads alongside amazing highways do not share a bridge to the heart of Christ and his love for justice.

In our desire to see justice, we must be willing to help restore the road. This "road" to which I refer includes the systems that keep people and often whole segments of society in brokenness. As

Christians we should be troubled by these systems, as God's heart is a heart of restoration. Where in the Bible do we see God leave people in a broken place? We must be agents of restoration who are willing to engage systemic injustice.

After a season in which our family of three lived in the transitional housing program, we moved to a single-family home. Child number two was on its way and we wanted to live in a house with a guaranteed place to park. Yes, that was one of my only desires: a driveway!

We moved to a low-income, predominantly immigrant neighborhood and reared our kids alongside families for which English was a second language and hard work and multiple jobs were a matter of survival. Living among immigrants not only opened my eyes to their hard work ethic, commitment to family, and vibrant culture but also began to highlight the limitations of our immigration system.

I became a student of immigration initially through relationship. I saw some families travel to Mexico for the summer while others only sent children; some never visited at all. When the media talked about immigration using words like "undocumented," this now represented people—my children's friends, my neighbors.

A young man in my community came to the United States when he was four years old. He attended the schools in our neighborhood, graduated from high school, and participated in one of our local church ministries, being mentored and supported for many years. He is what we often refer to as a "Dreamer"—an undocumented person who was brought here as a child by an adult.

During the young man's senior year of high school, he was driving with his father and younger brother and was pulled over for a broken taillight. After a series of events, his father was taken into custody and deported, separating the family. Because this young man and his mother had only crossed the border in the first place to join his father, after the father was deported, his mother and siblings left to go back to Mexico. As an eighteen-year-old he was left with a choice, and he chose to stay.

His reason was chilling. "My chances at a life in Mexico are very limited," he said. "A young man my age has only two options: join the military and fight the drug cartels or join the drug cartels and fight the military. I think I will take my chances and stay. Maybe something in the law will change."

Systemic injustice does not simply change. It starts with an awareness of brokenness and the commitment to repair or restore what is broken.

Transforming the Jericho Road

Calling out the brokenness of the Jericho road and its need to be restructured, Martin Luther King Jr., in a message at Riverside Church in New York in April 1967, referenced the need to engage public policy to eradicate the suffering of those whose journey is limited by brokenness:

> A true revolution of values will soon cause us to question the fairness and justice of many of our past and present policies. On the one hand, we are called to play the Good Samaritan on life's roadside, but that will be only an initial act. One day we must come to see that the whole Jericho Road must be transformed so that men and women will not be constantly beaten and robbed as they make their journey on life's highway. True compassion is more than flinging a coin to a beggar. It comes to see that an edifice which produces beggars needs restructuring.

Cleaning up the road and fixing its perils is not something we can accomplish through one- or two-day outreaches. It's not about making the road a more desirable place to live. Gentrification, which is happening in our cities all over the country, actually displaces broken people even further.

Gentrification is not restoration of the people on life's Jericho road or a solution to systemic injustice. It is a push-pull factor of the economic principle of supply and demand. It is recognizing that a broken place has the potential to be desirable to those who are fast enough, smart enough, and well-positioned enough to take it without feeling badly. It leads to an economic survival of the fittest, and you can pull up a chair with a number of my Native American friends and listen to what that has looked like in their history.

As someone who lives in a now nearly all gentrified city, I remember the day when it was nasty and not well-traveled by people like me. I am grateful for the cleanliness coming to our side of the tracks. I love hipster coffee shops and well-lit streets. I am glad our neighborhoods are safer and easier to walk, but I also know it has come at a cost for the people who originally lived here and for those who choose to travel with them. Together we have felt gentrification's impact through its camping bans, skyrocketing real estate costs, lawsuits that keep us from legally buying our way in and financially securing a place in our now renovated world.

Gentrification does clean up the road, but it does not help the beaten-up people lying along the side of it. They do not enter the new safe place but instead are pushed out so that the Levite and the priest don't have to worry about encountering them.

A chosen front-row seat to injustice enables us to stay focused on the work that needs to be done. It's okay to change. We need to expand our limited experience and understanding so that our perspective can change along with our heart and head. The journey toward justice requires that people traveling the highways and the

Jericho road work together to impact people and systems. The vision is so massive that it needs open-minded, timeless perspectives to bring forth realistic and appropriate solutions.

As you stay proximate, do not resist the transformational work that is happening to your heart and mind. Remember that God is much bigger than our ways of thinking and that his truths do not change (Isaiah 55:8), regardless of what happens with ours.

Chapter Three

EMBRACING BROKENNESS

*S*eeing and sharing the pain and injustice surrounding the poor doesn't just change our perspective and social construct and force us to dig deeper into our faith; it also changes our perception of our own wholeness and our ability to confront the brokenness around us. Working alongside brokenness has a way of revealing the deep brokenness and inadequacies of all humanity, which includes us, the ones who want to find solutions to the problems surrounding poverty and injustice.

I have never met anyone who works toward engaging injustice who thinks they have it all together. I have never met anyone who thinks they have nothing to offer either. Most people have studied hard trying to acquire experience and formal skills to support the work they want to do.

I was no different.

When I embarked on a life of ministry alongside the poor, I brought with me what I like to call my "big bag of Bible." While I am deeply committed to the teachings of the Bible, as I have already shared, much of what I had understood of God up to that point directly correlated to my experience. So I led from what I had experienced and understood.

When I would come across someone who needed "help," I would go into my bag of Bible training and throw whatever I could find at the situation. I looked at problems as cut-and-bandage situations instead of the gaping, bleeding arteries they were. My view of God and his salvation for our broken world was shallow and quick. I was an urban Santa with toys nobody knew what to do with—least of all myself.

It didn't take long for me to realize that what I was offering was not working. But I kept at it because I had no idea what else to do. Talk about insanity! I spent a long time throwing out the "goods" in my bag, until one day I realized the bag was empty. And you know what? I was so disillusioned with what I'd been offering that I wasn't even worried that I had nothing else to give. I was finally free to stop doing what I'd been taught to do—knowing full well it wasn't working. Somewhere in the midst of the pain of those who suffered I saw my own brokenness and limitedness. I was finally free to just be and do.

I had nothing left from my past and hadn't gained any solutions to replenish the bag—I simply had myself. I could offer myself and just quietly walk through the loneliness with people. I was free to listen without an answer or solution. I was able to grieve that there were no easy or fast solutions to the problems they faced and all we could do was pray for faith—faith to believe that what we hoped for would be enough to get us going together.

As a Christian justice advocate, I tell people that you cannot journey alongside broken people if you don't recognize your own brokenness. The reality is that *all* people are broken. Brokenness has a way of revealing brokenness.

Becoming Approachable

For some reason God decided it was a good idea to make me a physically weak person. He made up for my weakness in so many other ways that most people don't know I struggle with some serious health issues. But if you live alongside me there is no way you can avoid seeing my limitations.

Two of my major issues (I have a few) are rheumatoid arthritis and chronic pain. I have had bouts of inflammation that, in the past, lasted for years but have now become intermittent. One Sunday my inflammation was so severe that I had to use my forearm crutches to get around. I hate when this happens. Suffering silently I can handle, but having people see me hobbling around in pain invites them to talk to me about something I don't like to discuss: my physical weakness.

That day I hobbled into church, swallowing my pride, knowing I was inviting people to engage this issue of mine that I'd rather they forget. It had been a couple of years since I'd had to use crutches at church and the many people who surrounded me were exhausting. Yet knowing this was a good test of my patience, I pushed through the countless conversations. That night when we were at our community meal, I sat down, spent, and a man who was new to our church began to share with me about his own health issues, showing me his scars.

Later one of my friends stopped by and asked why I thought I was having trouble again. My answer? "I think God just wanted to give people an opportunity to connect with me and share their hurts."

Broken people are able to help broken people. If we are unwilling to see ourselves as among the broken, we miss the chance to travel together toward restoration.

I remember hearing my friend and colleague Noel Castellanos speak and share of his brokenness. He believes that God has accomplished more through his brokenness than through his wholeness. From my experience, that statement could not be more true, yet this is not something we often hear in our churches. God's mission is to rescue the world, because the world needs a Savior—the whole world, not just the poor. God invites us to join him in his efforts, but as we practice our theology in ministry, we catch his mission and realize just how much we ourselves need rescuing.

This is an essential part of gaining clarity into injustice. We need to get a realistic picture not only of what's going on in our society and how issues impact people, but how our own issues affect us. We have to stay with the poor long enough to walk alongside the road with them. As we remain proximate we get a front-row seat into our own brokenness.

When we were at the transitional house for homeless teens, we received some unexpected and unplanned news: we were expecting our second child—two years earlier than planned. Our first child was just eight months old.

Our carefully laid plans for our family went out the window. Starting and running a transitional home with one baby was already a lot of work, and it didn't take long for us to realize that two little ones seventeen months apart meant I needed to rethink my immediate ministry plans. So David and I began to look for replacements to run the house we had started not that long ago. God also used this time to move us forward with the idea of Open Door Ministries.

Not more than six weeks from the time we found out we were expecting, I miscarried the baby. Our hearts were broken. Though

I'd been overwhelmed at the prospect of all that change and adjustment, I wanted two babies at once. I grieved.

The night I miscarried the baby, Dave and I asked the girls in the house to please take care of themselves while we spent some quiet time alone together. It was a sad, sad night—and the girls definitely took care of themselves. While we were in another room with the door closed, one resident snuck into our bedroom and stole all my nice jewelry. My great-great-grandmother's wedding ring, earrings, necklaces—it was all gone. We noticed the theft the next morning after the girls had left for the day. We realized it had happened less than fifteen hours after I miscarried our baby. The girl who stole the jewelry never returned.

I got scared and angry at the same time. I ran upstairs to the girls' bedrooms and began to search for the jewelry, with no success. I knew it wasn't there. It hit me then that I had lost a baby, family gifts, and even heirlooms, and at that moment I yelled out in anger and kicked the wall. My foot went right through the wall, and the hole remained for years.

I was not proud of that hole or any of the host of emotional reactions I have had in the frustrating, sometimes exasperating work of doing justice along the Jericho road. But I'm glad it was a visual reminder to all the people who came after me; they would have their own breaking points, over and over again.

Pouring myself out for the poor and doing what I could did not work most of the time—and sometimes I even got robbed. It's a lie to pretend that this kind of thing doesn't kick you in the gut and reveal anger, disappointment, and disillusionment. It makes you dig deep and admit you are being affected by the pain and brokenness all around you. The journey toward our own restoration through pain and disappointment cannot be rushed, despite our attempts to hold it together pretending life is easy, good, and successful.

Reinforcing Redemption

The closer we get to the pain of others, the bigger and more unfixable their problems seem. The prospect of dealing with these problems is scary. It's scary because we don't have much to offer in terms of guarantees for the effectiveness of our ministry in their lives. It's scary because of the chaos we experience in our own thoughts and how this plays into our fears and inadequacies.

We become proximate to make a difference. If people have problems I can't fix, then I am not making a difference and all my sacrifices are worthless. And then all those people who told me I shouldn't live in proximity to the poor were right. I should have stayed home in my homogenous silo.

It's often at this stage of realization that I see people begin to fade away into other careers instead of leaning in. Disillusionment sets in and we drift off, refusing to stay long enough to allow the redemption message we were so eager to share to be practiced in our own lives. But the experience of redemption alongside those who are broken strengthens the individual and collective voices of the body in affirming that God turns ashes to beauty (Isaiah 61:1-3).

The Chosen by Chaim Potok is the story of two young Jewish boys in Brooklyn near the end of World War II. One of the book's major themes is the impact of suffering on a person's heart. One of the two boys is the brilliant son of an Orthodox rabbi who has chosen to rear his son "in silence." The father speaks only of faith to the boy and nothing else. This choice not to speak is the father's attempt to help his son gain compassion for others. He realizes that empathy does not come naturally for his son, who plans to be a rabbi like him. As the story concludes, we finally hear why the father has chosen this path, as well as the pain it has caused the father to practice this form of parenting:

> One learns of the pain of others by suffering one's own pain
> . . . by turning inside oneself, by finding one's own soul. And
> it is important to know of pain. . . . It destroys our self-pride,
> our arrogance, our indifference toward others. It makes us
> aware of how frail and tiny we are and of how much we must
> depend on the Master of the Universe.

Embracing our own fragility enables us to run to the One whose grace is made perfect in our weakness, whose life exemplified an attitude of humility and the need to deeply depend on God.

Jesus left his place in heaven to come share life alongside us. God incarnate came to save the world. Paul wrote his epistle to the Philippians during his first imprisonment (he was imprisoned while serving God!), and while it is mostly a letter of encouragement and a warning against false teachers, it also warns about pride and self-seeking attitudes that can be destructive:

> Do nothing out of selfish ambition or vain conceit. Rather, in
> humility value others above yourselves. . . .
>
> In your relationships with one another, have the same
>   mindset as Christ Jesus:
> Who, being in very nature God,
>   did not consider equality with God something to
> be used to his own advantage;
> rather, he made himself nothing
>   by taking the very nature of a servant,
>   being made in human likeness.
> And being found in appearance as a man,
>   he humbled himself
>   by becoming obedient to death—
>   even death on a cross! (Philippians 2:3-8)

Just as Christ emptied himself to come restore what was broken by sin here on earth, we as his followers need to have the same attitude and willingly empty ourselves of our demands, privileges, and perspectives of wholeness to join the poor and share in solidarity of presence—not because they can't live without us but because we cannot live without them.

A commitment to social justice ministry and restorative action will reveal that we are not the ones who can fix problems. We are simply the ones who share the journey, offering what we have and allowing God to transform us in the process.

We need a deep relationship with Christ to sustain us and give us an ability to see beyond the immediate. We need to allow God to show us how his grace is perfected in weakness and how he uses even our lowest points of despair to bring about the personal restoration needed for the bigger challenges around the bend.

Peter was one of Jesus' most well-known apostles. A fisherman by trade, he followed Christ without reserve and was near him throughout his ministry on earth. On Jesus' last night with his disciples, during the Last Supper, he revealed that everyone there would scatter and leave him, but after he arose he would meet up with them again.

Peter confidently replied, "Even if all fall away on account of you, I never will." At that moment Jesus leaned in and told Peter that not only would he leave Jesus; he would deny him three times on that same night. Indignant at the preposterous accusation, Peter declared, "Even if I have to die with you, I will never disown you!" (Matthew 26:31-35).

Jesus' prediction came true and Peter did precisely what he said he would not—three times. After he realized what he had done, he went outside and "wept bitterly" (Matthew 26:75).

I can identify closely with Peter. He had such good intentions. He wanted to believe he was strong enough and would never do something disloyal to the one who had called him to help establish a new kingdom.

I don't think Peter wept simply because he had failed in that moment; I think he wept because he had come so far and grown so much, been a part of so much change and seen so much restoration, that he was grieved to learn he was not the man he thought he was. Even more than that, he wasn't the man he'd hoped he could be.

Proximity not only reveals who we are but also allows us to fail miserably. We come to see that we are not the people we thought we were or even hoped we would be. This is a grief but also a necessary process.

The story of Peter's reunion with the resurrected Christ finds him on a beach before Jesus' ascension. They go back and forth with a question-and-answer dialogue. Jesus: "Peter, do you love me?" Peter: "Jesus, you know I love you" (see John 21:15-19). All the while Jesus affirms Peter's ability to move on from what seemed like the ultimate blow to his life of service for Christ.

All of this brokenness and inadequateness was a precursor for the apostle Peter, whose subsequent life and witness were lifted up for all to see. He was a warrior for the gospel, mistakes and all, who was restored over and over again, faithfully serving Christ and his body until his death.

Wounded Healers

Henri Nouwen was a Catholic priest who wrote many books about spiritual life. I found *The Wounded Healer* most helpful when learning about the role of a minister in relation to one's own brokenness. Nouwen writes:

> A minister is not a doctor whose primary task is to take away pain. Rather, he deepens the pain to a level where it can be shared. . . . Ministry is a very confronting service. It does not

allow people to live with illusions of immortality and wholeness. It keeps reminding others that they are mortal and broken, but also that with the recognition of this conditions, liberation starts.

In subsequent pages Nouwen speaks about community and how it is birthed when pain is shared, "not as a stifling form of self-complaint, but as a recognition of God's saving promises."

He also stresses that we must be willing to search for as authentic a posture as possible, not as a person watching someone's pain from the sideline, not taking a position or even as "an impartial observer, but as an articulate witness of Christ, who puts his own search at the disposal of others."

Nouwen clarifies this search placed at the disposal of others as hospitality, or the opening of one's heart. He says this requires the minister to draw boundaries but also that it allows "others to enter his life, come close to him and ask him how their lives connect with his."

Nouwen concludes that there is no way to anticipate where this will lead each time. Opening our heart and world to brokenness is risky because we never know what impact the other person will have.

There must be a careful balance between sharing life alongside broken people and sharing our own brokenness. This balance, not easy to achieve, can be sought in counsel from more experienced, mature people who are journeying alongside us. Searching for authenticity by allowing others to enter our life, to come close and make connections, leaves us vulnerable and exposed. But as Nouwen shares, "It is exactly in common searches and shared risks that new ideas are born, that new visions reveal themselves and that new roads become visible." We learn of our own brokenness as we gain clarity—not just in seeing issues clearly but in seeing ourselves clearly. And that observation can be the hardest to embrace.

Bryan Stevenson, a respected lawyer, scholar, author, and speaker as well as founder and director of the Equal Justice Initiative, shares in his book *Just Mercy* his own realization of personal brokenness when he worked alongside incarcerated people and their families:

> For the first time I realized that my life was just full of brokenness. I worked in a broken system of justice. My clients were broken by mental illness, poverty, and racism. They were torn apart by disease, drugs and alcohol, pride, fear and anger.
>
> In their broken state, they were judged and condemned by people whose commitment to fairness had been broken by cynicism, hopelessness and prejudice.
>
> Being close to suffering, death, executions and cruel punishment didn't just illuminate the brokenness of others, in a moment of anguish and heartbreak, it also exposed my own brokenness. You cannot effectively fight abusive power, poverty, inequality, illness, oppression and injustice and not be broken by it.... But, our shared brokenness connected us.

Stevenson, coming to grips with the reality of brokenness on all sides—from assailants to victims to the system to himself—came to the realization that we all at some point need to address: our choice in engaging it all.

Those of us who choose proximity to the poor are faced with a choice when we see what's really in the world and in our own hearts: "We can embrace our humanness, which means embracing our broken natures and the compassion that remains our best hope for healing. Or we can deny our brokenness, forswear compassion and as a result deny our own humanity."

Gaining clarity over time into our own soul and the reasons why we're doing what we're doing is important work. Embracing our pain and weakness exposes our soul, our limitations, our inadequacies.

We think we're finished with nothing else to give and something inside screams, "*Run!*" That's when we choose to whisper back, "Stay," and more clearly see brokenness in its raw state.

The sun came up again the morning after we lost our baby and I lost my jewelry. A couple of days later the exhaustion and anger began to subside. As I cried out to God for healing and help, he not only met me where I was but began to breathe words of comfort, hope, and perseverance into me. The commitment to move forward was so strong that when David went to look for the girl, now back on the street, I remember calling out to him, pleading, "Tell her I forgive her and that she can reapply to come back in thirty days."

This response is not a human act. This is the Holy Spirit revealing that the actions of a young, homeless girl living on the streets, desperate enough to take something from another in their pain, scream of an even deeper brokenness in need of restoration.

When things happen around us, we are left with a choice to embrace the agenda of God and give our broken, poor-in-spirit, weary selves to the master of the universe who fills us with dreams, hopes, and ideals that are linked to his dreams, hopes, and ideals for his children. We need a deep relationship with Christ to sustain us and give us the ability to see beyond the immediate. We need to allow God to show us how his grace is perfected in weakness (2 Corinthians 12:9) and how he uses even our lowest points of despair to bring about the personal restoration needed for the bigger challenges around the bend.

Clarity into the Problem

One of the hardest things to do when we begin to learn about pain and injustice, especially when someone we know is directly impacted, is to stay on the sidelines. The desire to jump in and "fix" is part of our American social construct. The United States is the superpower of the world, so we must also assume the role of superhero and rescue everyone with our knowledge, insight, wealth, and experience.

I have seen it in people who come to my community to help serve for a short time. The last thing I want to do is criticize those of our body who come to share a moment in their week, summer, or season and make them think their presence is not welcomed. But I do want to clarify that people are not problems in need of fixing. People, including us, have problems that call for shared journeying.

It is also hard for those of us who do stay for a longer season in proximity bearing witness to the struggle not to jump in quickly to "solve" or "fix" problems. Life should work and move forward, right? Yet for those trapped in systemic injustice, the timeline is slow, which is a significant part of the struggle. The poor and powerless are often disregarded, and it takes time to do justice alongside them. Even after we have had some of our perspective reshaped and our social construct deconstructed, the time we must spend building together is long.

Bearing witness to the pain people endure can become maddening. Our inability to affect it within a specific time frame is out of sync with our results-driven culture. But in the waiting, we begin to see beyond individual pain in the moment and collective pain in the immediate past to the bigger systemic issues at the core. This enables us to address it more effectively and completely.

No one wants to paint, furnish, and move a family into a home with a foundation that is ready to crumble. "Helpers" who get the surface-level job done, take some pictures, and go back to life feeling good about the new paint and furniture are not actually helping. We need to step back and be willing to do the hard foundational work, all the time realizing that the immediate needs of a family to be housed cannot go unmet.

Even long-term, up-close proximity to pain and injustice doesn't provide the complete picture. There are always underlying issues, and each time we pull away one layer, we find another. We need to remain proximate to humanity and its ills so we become better informed. Our tendency—if not to run away entirely—is to cry "Injustice!" instead of cultivating a deeper understanding of all that is in play.

Since we in the pragmatic evangelical world work so hard to achieve results for our efforts, we often don't slow down enough to truly understand the complexities of the issues. Even while people's futures hang in the balance and we bear witness, it is still imperative that we understand that proximity gives us space and time to see the depth of what is going on. I know it's hard. How can we stand on the sidelines when we see something broken? How can we watch people continue to suffer and not aggressively move forward?

I am not a proponent of waiting; I am a proponent of listening and of learning.

Those of us who have chosen proximity to the poor have a different lens when we view how the world works. When we begin to learn about how others are impacted by injustice, it's hard not to jump in quickly. It's also hard to wait and learn about the people and the deeper stories behind what is happening. The reality is the more we know alongside people, the better we can respond collectively.

We cannot fix a problem we don't understand. Much systemic injustice is housed in racist systems. While I will interface with the issue of racism in subsequent chapters, the reality is that many of our systems are based on racist biases, and unless you are a person of color, you will never understand the problem truly. You cannot fix it. You cannot understand it. The strongest voices of injustice are those directly impacted. We must learn to listen, learn, and follow their insights.

Listening, Learning, and Following

Assuming you have followed me so far, you know that moving to a proximate place helps us see injustice more clearly. However, before we respond to it, we need to understand that those who are impacted by injustice are the primary teachers of the struggle. We need to listen and learn directly from those affected and allow them not only to teach us of its impact but set the direction for the issues they want to work on. When we allow them to teach us and invite us to join their efforts, then we can help *them* fix the problem.

Following the lead of others is challenging for individualistic, solution-focused problem solvers who come from the privileged, pragmatic evangelical church like myself. I left my place of privilege to become proximate, and instead of working to quickly cross injustice off my to-do list, I have had to wait and learn more from those who are directly impacted. But I just want to "do" something.

I remember some years ago working to recruit local Denver leaders to focus on the issue of mass incarceration. We were trying to collectively join the Christian Community Development Association's (CCDA's) national awareness and action day called Locked in Solidarity. This annual event is designed to bring people together to share stories, Scripture, and statistics around mass incarceration, enabling those directly impacted by the issue to share and articulate their experience, speaking to broader systemic issues.

These leaders I had been working with were all proximate to the pain of those affected by incarceration; they were the "real deal" as far as loving their neighbor as themselves. Many of them were highly experienced. But one leader was newer to the scene. His passion for the community was not only admirable but needed. His idealistic understanding of engaging systemic injustice was typical of those who are newer to issues that need a sustained response.

Mass incarceration is a reality people in our communities deal with every day. Mothers watch their sons go to prison; children grow up without parents. Our friends have all either been behind bars or are related to those who have been or are. The need to change mandatory minimum sentences, drug scheduling, over-policing of schools, and other issues related to mass incarceration is dire. People's lives are impacted greatly by these policies. We need to *do* something.

It is maddening for those of us in proximity to see friends get beaten up by police, receive the harshest of sentences, and spend much of their adult lives behind bars for crimes others would walk away from with limited consequences. The incarceration system disproportionately impacts low-income communities of color—the kinds of neighborhoods where the leaders putting together Locked in Solidarity live. Those of us from the outside who have to bear witness to this can become frantic about making change quickly.

We were getting ready to hold a prayer rally, and the idea of praying seemed like a cliché response to our newer leader. He wrote an email to all of us that referenced not wanting to fight a battle but win a war. His rally cry was to see if we could put our collective leadership efforts toward one big issue in the mass incarceration issue. He wasn't as interested in slow work that showed few results such as this event.

I don't blame him. I wish there was a silver bullet solution to this systemic injustice thing. Once you become aware of an injustice, it's hard not to want to move quickly to try to fix it. I have seen it in myself as well as in the countless people who have chosen to live and work in proximity in my community. I have also seen it in those who have lived among the injustice for their entire lives. Sometimes it's hard to believe anything can or will change.

Overcoming our own haste and others' skepticism is the place where advocates and organizers like me live. Do people have the resources to engage the issue I am seeing? Is this where we want to spend our energy? Will this effort do any lasting good? Will our engagement build or burn bridges for the future? Who's leading: me or the person impacted by the injustice? Are we doing it together?

Deep systemic problems do not get fixed with a single solution. Systemic injustice is layered in such deep ways that changing it requires careful, sustained observation and a calculated response for the long haul. If it took a thousand bullets to make the holes in the fence, it's going to take time to rebuild it and make things right.

While that night's prayer event didn't do much to change the immediate injustices around mass incarceration, the stories and experiences shared by my friends helped me see aspects of the broken system and people's pain in ways I had not known before. I am and will always be learning.

That evening my friend of years shared about her son who was in prison for life. She talked about his father before him being in prison for life as well. As the mother of a black son, she knows firsthand how incarceration affects families. She shared about what it's like to be a low-income mother hours away from her son in a faraway prison. She talked about how expensive the gas was, how long it took to get there in a car that barely worked. She talked of having hungry kids in tow since no outside food was allowed in the prison and the high price of the vending machines that were their only option on visiting days. She talked about trying to stay in touch by phone between visits but how the prices to place a call were exorbitant and the minute-by-minute cost unattainable by poor families whose relatives were disproportionately behind bars.

I listened to her stories and others' whose details I hadn't known because I hadn't created space for this conversation until now. For years, my friend and I had held each other in tearful embraces at holidays and birthdays when she was separated from her boy. We had shared court dates and prayer requests, years of history and hopes for the future, but I did not know about any of this.

I was reminded again that day, as I am many days when I listen and learn from people in my world, that I am limited in my understanding even though proximate. I still have much to learn about the impact of incarceration, race, poverty, and addiction on the everyday experiences of my neighbors. One of the strongest ways to love my neighbors is to listen to them, learn from their experiences and insights, and follow their lead as we journey toward change together.

Slowing Down for Lament

Moving fast might make us feel like we are "doing" something to engage injustice, but studying and learning allow for a deeper awareness. Wanting quick action can come from a good place. We all want to eradicate injustice. Winning the "war" would be a great victory. And we want the pain to stop—everyone's pain, including ours. Nobody should hurt, not those who are directly suffering nor those who have to bear witness to it. Nobody should have to cry or be in pain, but they do and they are. And while we wait for God's restoration, we need to sit in the pain and practice lament.

We see lament practiced in the psalms and the books of prophecy, yet we as Christians in America—especially privileged America—

are not taught this discipline. We have been taught that we should celebrate God's goodness and all-sufficient grace. We don't want to cry, weep, or suffer for long if at all; it's as if we think this is not part of God's story for us.

In his book *Prophetic Lament*, Soong-Chan Rah speaks of burying the practice of lament alongside our worship. In regard to our views of social justice engagement he states this:

> The term *justice* is too casually thrown about without the corresponding sacrifice. We want the popularity associated with being justice activists, but we don't want to lament alongside those who suffer. Instead of a justice that arises from the lament of suffering, justice is misappropriated as a furtherance of the narrative of celebration. American Christian justice leaders are applauded for their self-sacrifice, which allows for a furtherance of the Western exceptionalism and even an exploitation of justice as a career-building move. The uplifting of privileged individuals who use justice to expand their own influence serves a narrative of triumphalism rather than engaging the narrative of lament. There are too many examples of justice misappropriated and even thwarted.

The process of understanding people's pain, sharing it, and joining them in their struggle, cannot be rushed. If we do, we will miss the transformation of our proximate place. Not only are we unable to fix a problem we don't understand; no one can fix systemic injustice alone. We need others with us and a collection of voices to share the journey, and that is good news for the body of Christ.

Remaining Steadfast

As we remain proximate, bearing witness and learning from people directly impacted by injustice, we are ready to move beyond awareness to action. But this is not an easy step to take. As I have lived in proximity I find it difficult to look at the pain closely. It's hard to admit that things happen to people the way they do. It can be tempting to believe in the goodness and easiness of the world from which I came. I am tempted to go back to living for myself. But as hard as it is, how can I do anything but lean into love and engage?

As we close out this section on proximity changing and informing our perspective, I want to reference the disciples and how they were asked to look at their next steps of engagement in their chosen proximity to live with and follow Christ.

In John 6 Jesus has just fed five thousand people and walked on water when he begins teaching about his being the bread of life. It's a major high point for the disciples since crowds are following Jesus in swarms. Then, in an effort to better explain who he is and what it means to truly follow him, Jesus starts to teach about the covenant relationship of eating his flesh and drinking his blood. The words are strange to those who have been following Jesus, and the unfamiliar teaching causes many to turn away and stop following him.

As people drift off because what they're learning is too hard to digest, Jesus turns to the twelve disciples and asks, "Are you also going to leave?" (John 6:67 NLT). Peter is the first to respond. I resonate with Peter's response to that question, but before I mention what he says, I need to give you a little background into Peter's story of following Jesus.

The story (see Luke 5:1-11) starts with Peter and other fishermen washing their nets after a night of unsuccessful fishing. In an effort to find a place to teach effectively, Jesus climbs in one of the boats and asks Peter to push out a little so he can sit and teach the crowds from just offshore. Peter does what Jesus asks.

After the preaching time is over, instead of asking Peter to row for shore, Jesus tells him to push out farther and begin fishing again. After some arguing about the unsuccessful work of the night before, Peter obeys, makes the catch of his life, sees that he has had an encounter with God, pulls his boat up on the shore, leaves everything, and follows Jesus!

Peter left his familiar life not to follow a dream but to follow Jesus. He believed that Jesus was the way, the truth, and the life. Yet I am sure that what he experienced was hard for him to understand and engage with at times.

Jesus asked Peter and the other disciples to do some non-Jewish-type things, including eating with seedy characters and standing up to powerful leaders, all the while affirming Peter's commitment to follow him. I have no doubt that the community Peter left to follow Christ so radically wondered if he was losing his mind, becoming a liberal, or forsaking the faith. But Peter decided to stay and engage even when the messages were hard to understand. Some were so shocking they even caused people to turn away from Jesus—or at least follow him from a safer, less risky distance.

Not Peter. There he stands, watching others walk away disillusioned. Then Jesus asks him, "Are you going to leave too?"

Peter's response, much like my own so many times when I hear hard things I don't understand or watch people walk away, is this: "Lord, to whom would we go? You have the words that give eternal life. We believe, and we know you are the Holy One of God" (John 6:68-69 NLT).

In that sacred space of knowing people's pain and the fullness of a life with Christ amidst injustice, I find myself too "in" to leave.

Where would I go? What would I do with the things I know now? I have no place in which to return.

When we reach this place, proximity to the poor has begun its deep transformational work. We have gained a deeper awareness of our own souls and those impacted by poverty and injustice, which not only transforms the way we think but the way we engage. Filled with a stronger sense of awareness we are compelled to move toward action—action that is defined by Christ's love.

Part Two

PROXIMITY
COMPELS RESPONSE

Chapter Four

LEANING INTO LOVE

What are you going to do with what you know? It's a question I perpetually ask myself and those that I journey with. Sometimes I feel like I know and have experienced too much, and thinking about what to do with it affords me the opportunity to be brave and lean into love—or shut down and quit.

Learning in proximity about the pain and injustice of the poor goes beyond simple awareness and compels a deeper response. In our Christian society today, our natural tendency when we learn of injustice is to begin to talk about it. This is an essential starting point, but it is not the end; it is hardly even the beginning.

There is no lack of conferences, seminars, TED talks, or Q talks in our churches and institutions designed to teach us about injustice around the world, providing us with platforms to talk about what we are learning. It's good to learn and we need these conversations. But then what?

Talking about injustice is of little value unless it drives us to deeper engagement. Talk is easy, which is why it's cheap and personally costs us so little. "Liking" something on Facebook does not take much effort. Doing something with what we know is much more difficult.

Growing up in my home I frequently heard the phrase "To whom much is given, much is required." My parents, not far from their own humble, immigrant heritage, knew we had many resources and opportunities at our disposal. Their expectation was that we would not simply slide through our life but multiply our resources. Because eventually, when our time was over, we would have to give an account of what we did or did not do with what we had.

This phrase of my childhood, proverbial in nature, actually comes from the Gospels. Jesus, in Luke 12:47, tells his followers that they need to be watchful and realize that this world with its offerings is a temporal place. God is going to return and we need to be ready. As Jesus shares this message of waiting and watching with the crowds, he's ensuring that they get the message that they are responsible to do something with what they've been given, including the time they have here on earth. "From everyone who has been given much, much will be demanded; and from the one who has been entrusted with much, much more will be asked" (Luke 12:48).

In essence, we are responsible for what we have. The more we have, the more we are responsible for; those of us from the privileged church cannot just build our lives, learn about pain, and hope Jesus comes back soon. We need to invest in his kingdom with our time here on earth before he comes back, knowing we will be held responsible for what we do with what we know.

Sitting on our opportunities, storing them up for ourselves, is not the response of a Christian disciple. Our individual and collective resources are to be shared. It's not about playing a game with the government and our taxes—trying to keep as much for ourselves through every loophole we can exploit. Our lives and what we are given are to be given back in service to the world, just as Jesus gave his life in service to the world.

Jesus, the Word, Proximate to Us

The story of Jesus becoming proximate to us is an amazing narrative. Because of sin the Trinity wove together a plan to reconcile the world back to God. Members of the Trinity came together, talked about what they would do, and then took action on the ultimate demonstration of love.

We learn in Philippians that Jesus did not think he was too great to leave heaven, put himself in the humble position of humanity, and become obedient to sacrifice (Philippians 2:5-8). We also learn from this passage that we should have the same attitude as Christ. We should be willing to leave our communities of comfort to choose a proximate place and humbly and sacrificially follow Christ's example of love.

Learning of the pain of others can compel us to become proximate, which should move us to engage more deeply. The more we know as a result of our chosen proximity, the more we have the opportunity to put our words—our "talk"—into action.

This shouldn't be a big stretch for Christians who follow Jesus. Our ultimate example refers to himself as the Word of Life or simply the Word. The Word became flesh and did something (John 1:14). His words directly correlated to his action. He brought good news to the poor, fully extending his love in his death, providing us a way to be reconciled to God. His chosen proximate place was to be born into the world a pauper and die a criminal's death. All of this for us. His proximity had purpose. Our proximity needs to have purpose as well.

Christian discipleship is far from easy because it is a choice to leave what you know and follow Christ to an unfamiliar place. Remember the story of Peter and how he left everything to follow Christ?

The Choice to Walk into the Unfamiliar

Have you ever talked about doing something so much that when you got to the point of actually doing it, you wanted to change your mind? Story of my life. I can easily feel passionate about something, talk it up, convince people to join me, and then, when it's ready to happen, feel like I am about to pass out for fear of actually doing it!

Walking the Jericho road with its front-row view into the life of the poor, riddled with brokenness and stagnation, has often felt very lonely. I have often been caught between two worlds and felt disillusioned with both. The world I left has ever beckoned me to return, and the life I have pushed into has repeatedly made evident my inadequacies to address life-and-death problems that need to be resolved.

Before I became proximate to the poor, I lived in what I will refer to as a beautiful, manicured English garden. You can picture it in your mind—lovely shrubs shaped to perfection, clear paths all surrounded by a large hedge on every side. But one day I felt like I needed to move outward from the familiar garden, beyond what I knew and understood. I was being beckoned to an unfamiliar place, and I began to talk about this new awareness that was drawing me to engage more deeply until one day it was time to leave and put this new awareness into action.

At that moment it was like someone handed me a big machete and told me to go make a life for myself beyond the hedge. At first it sounded fun and adventurous, so I hacked away at what I saw and moved forward. As I ventured into what was now a jungle, paralyzing and invasive, I could still look back to the garden and see the familiar comforts of home.

The insecure feeling of leaving the familiar behind was mounting as I leaned into the jungle and continued to forge a path. I knew I could still run back at any time, and that gave me some comfort. But the farther I went in, the more I began to understand my place in this unfamiliar jungle. The brush, up close to my face, no longer scared me but became familiar. My inability to see in front of me or around the corner became a way of life. One day I realized I could no longer see the path to the well-manicured garden. The journey was so far and long it didn't seem worth it to try to return, and even more startling was how comfortable I was in the closeness of the jungle and in my inability to see in front of my face.

I share this because it's easy to play it safe. It's easy to get scared when you get in deep and your world changes in ways that make it hard to return. It can make you want to change your mind. Please don't do it. We need you. The kingdom needs you. There are many lies out there trying to convince you to head back, but fight the lies. Be willing to forge ahead into the unfamiliar. Follow the example of Christ and his love and decide to push on—not as a martyr but as a disciple.

"The cost of discipleship" is a phrase we hear in church from the time we pray the sinner's prayer until forever. In essence it's the entire purpose of the church. Christ calls us to follow him, not to talk about following him or other people who follow him. We aren't supposed to follow people who talk about following Christ on Instagram or Twitter. We are supposed to follow him, put it into action, and engage.

Jesus' call to follow him does not lead us down a road that is easy and easily seen. The road is narrow and is marked by submission. We cannot have two lives. If we try to keep a foot in our former life and a foot in our proximate life, we will not have the abundant life God promises to those who follow him.

Worthless Idols

I didn't follow Christ to my proximate place out of fear but instead was compelled by his example of love. Sure, I had fears about the future, but following him was about faith. I trusted that he was going to lead me to a full life in him.

It's interesting to me how many young people talk to me about how their future children's lives will be affected if they choose to live a life of proximity to the poor. They understand the significance of choices that affect them and their future. They are concerned about implicating their children in those choices and fear that their decisions will reflect the opposite of love. They're concerned that they're setting their kids up for a miserable childhood.

Before I share some of my thinking behind my choices about my kids' futures, I want to at least say this: parenting is all about choosing courage instead of fear. I am one of four and my husband is one of four. Between the two of us we have six additional siblings and they have spouses and children. Twelve adults parenting a total of eighteen children. They all live in safe neighborhoods, have their kiddos in good schools, and attend churches with middle income or higher economic security.

And you know what? They worry and are afraid for their kids. It simply comes with the job of parenting. No matter where you choose to live you will be concerned about the choices you make and the choices they make. I am not the exception to this and neither are they. You cannot control the future well-being of your kids no matter where they are reared.

Of course to deny that I was concerned about my children would be a lie. This is something I thought about before I had kids and even afterward. Parenting in general is an insecure place filled with worries about what you do or don't do and who your kids will or will not grow up to be.

The summer we decided we would begin to start a family, I began to think more deeply about the choices we were making and how they would affect not only our future but that of our hoped-for children. Our talk of living and rearing children in this explicitly broken culture upped the ante, and our work to love and live in the community was about to take on some serious commitment.

I had been reading the Minor Prophets that summer, and while I was meditating on them I came across something in the book of Jonah I had never seen before. After Jonah had been in the belly of the whale, he prayed this little nugget that caught my eye and heart: "Those who cling to worthless idols turn away from God's love for them" (Jonah 2:8).

Our choice to bring our children into this proximate place began in me a journey of holding out what God would call "worthless idols" for me.

I was completely convicted by that verse in light of our impending decision to have children. I had to confess before the Lord that safe neighborhoods, successful schools, polished church programs, amazing musical performances, garage doors and openers, and other upper-middle-class amenities would not be part of my story or the story of my children. I cried and grieved all over again about the future loss, telling Jesus that if those were "worthless idols," then I would walk away from them again and again to gain a grace I would not have otherwise.

This was not a one-time decision before my daughter entered my womb; this was a daily painful decision every time we learned of another way that our children—there ended up being three of them—would have a life different from my own and my husband's. This was beyond hard. These were the conversations that brought David and me to our greatest disagreements. Not just me versus him, but the very calls on both our lives.

But the grace! Oh my, the grace that I had not known I would experience. Yes, my new community was different from the one I had grown up in. My children have received love, forgiveness, and a sense of togetherness I never knew existed. In my proximate place, there is no reason to live in a silo of individualism. Every failure and success is shared collectively.

My daughter's college essay began with this sentence: "I was reared by a community off of Colfax." Colfax is the largest state highway in the country and goes right through the center of Denver's downtown. It has been referred to as the wickedest, most sinful street in America. We started our ministry life in Denver living a few doors down from its nightlife. Yet beautiful things come from ashes and the most ironic places.

The words of that essay reinforce what I am trying to say—my kids grew up with a strong sense of community. When they succeed, we all succeed. When they fail, we all grieve. It has been and continues to be a beautiful life.

Sincerely Love

For years I led Open Door Ministries' summer internship program. This six- to eight-week summer program was filled with young people who looked similar to me when I arrived at my teaching job fresh out of college those many years ago. Our hope in this program was that interns would experience something of life in proximity and gain some experiences and training that would support a foundation for future work alongside the poor. Not everyone came in with a desire to live and work among the poor as a life's calling, but all left challenged to think about it and consider joining the good Christian justice work happening for Christ's kingdom throughout the world.

Every week we would have classes about life at Open Door, its history and ministries. We'd talk about theology and how it filtered through what we were learning. We talked about growing through stress, God's justice, our experience, systemic injustice, and the like. We would take the summer to meditate on Romans 12. This passage starts out talking about living as sacrifices, moves to service in the body of Christ, and ends with what love looks like in action. This chapter is a great place to dwell when you are learning about proximate living. "Don't think of yourself more highly than you ought to think." "Honor one another above yourself." "Share with the Lord's people who are in need." "Practice hospitality." "Live in harmony with one another." "Do not be proud but be willing to associate with people of low position." On and on this chapter goes calling us at the end to not be "overcome by evil but to overcome evil with good."

While every line of this chapter holds strong thoughts and reflections, the challenge in the first part of Romans 12:9 has always caught my attention. Paul tells us that "love must be sincere." We are often told to love in the Bible, but here love, which is often demonstrated in action, is challenged to be sincere.

I think one reason this has caught my attention is that I'm pretty good at looking like I love someone. I can pretend to enjoy something or someone for a really long time. Basically I can be a really good fake. A lifetime of being proximate has been good for me because I can't pretend to make it through this life. I cannot wait anything out. It's such a real place that my love, which is challenged to be sincere, can't be masked as "fake."

The process of learning to love sincerely is also a process that we never master completely. All of our actions can be considered a form of love. We act either out of sincere love that cares for the other person, or narcissism, a self-love that asks for something in return. It's easy for Christian stewards to get trapped into thinking we're doing the former when actually what we're doing has the latter all wrapped up inside it. Love of reputation is dangerous but easy to fall into when we are sacrificing personal gain, writing statistics, outcomes, and support letters, talking to volunteers, and so on. I want people to value what I do. I want them to give to the ministry I am involved in.

If we are going to demonstrate love in a sincere way, we need to better understand the heart of Christ and his perfect, sacrificial love.

Agape Love

Not having studied Greek, I am constantly learning from those who have. I have heard years' worth of sermons about love and know that there are four words for love in the Greek used throughout the New Testament. The three most familiar and commonly used words are *erōs*, *philia*, and *agapē*. Eros is an erotic, romantic love that refers to physical expressions of love. When people talk about having "chemistry," this is what they are referring to. Philia is a companionable type of love that can be felt for a person or something for which we have an affinity: "I love the ocean." Agape love is an unconditional, sacrificial love that gives itself without expecting or guaranteeing anything in return.

When Paul tells us to love sincerely in Romans 12:9, he is using the Greek word *agapē*. He is calling the body of Christ to an unconditional, sacrificial love without expecting a return on our investment. This is the love that Jesus constantly demonstrated to us.

In 1 John 3:16-18, we are told the very definition of love: "This is how we know what love [*agapē*] is: Jesus Christ laid down his life for us. And we ought to lay down our lives for our brothers and sisters. If anyone has material possessions and sees a brother or sister in need but has no pity on them, how can the love of God be in that person? Dear children, let us not love with words or speech but with actions and in truth."

The essence of Christ's agape love compels us to see people in need and respond with action and not simply talk. "My command is this: Love each other as I have loved you. Greater love has no one than this: to lay down one's life for one's friends" (John 15:12-13). Jesus left us to love—sacrificially. He said, "By this everyone will know that you are my disciples, if you love one another" (John 13:35). The signature of a Christian's life is love—sincere love, not self-love, love that feels pain and has no guarantees but hopes that God is good and we are not journeying alone.

Loving the Broken

Loving sincerely with great investment takes a miracle, which is why it is solely a result of the fruit of the Holy Spirit (Galatians 5:22). One of the most influential leaders in my life, one who actively demonstrates a life of loving the broken sacrificially, is Andy Cannon. Andy invited David and me to join the Open Door community back in 1995, and we are still living life together today. Andy is my spiritual father. Week after week, whether preaching at our church, sitting across from someone at a coffee shop, or sitting in hours and hours of meetings, Andy has exuded the sacrificial love of Christ in his life. Under his leadership I have watched his love and forgiveness toward people and institutions, and this has radically shaped the way I see and interact with people. Andy is one of those leaders who probably lets people off the hook too easily, and while I may wish he had been more stern a time or two with others, there have also been many times when his love, grace, and forgiveness have been extended to me when I needed a harsh rebuke.

Andy's memoir is *Loving the Broken: Following God's Heart into Compassionate Living.* There he records his journey as a young adult in the big-tent revival days in the South, when he lived in community with others from the Jesus Movement, until he found himself proximate to the broken, homeless, and addicted on East Colfax in downtown Denver. Andy is known for a lot of things, but most resoundingly he is known for his heart of love for broken people, of whom I am one. When I asked him to share what he has learned about loving the broken, he said,

> I have learned that there is no substitute for a life invested in a life. Arm's-length love and care is valuable, but life-on-life investment to the point of personal inconvenience and sacrifice is the model of Jesus and his disciples.

God's Mission to Rescue the World

Many years ago when I was looking more deeply into theology and the role of the ever-forming church, I was introduced to the works of Robert Webber. Webber wrote the Ancient-Future series, and as a worship leader who wanted to move more deeply into historical practices and incorporate liturgy and the Christian calendar, I found Webber's series, especially *Ancient-Future Time,* to be food for a hungry soul.

As I read through Webber's writings, practicing the Christian calendar in my personal life and then moving it into our corporate worship experience on Sundays, my theology in practice was challenged. Webber's book *The Younger Evangelicals* (which described me at the time) began to tap into a larger narrative than my simple, proximate life reflected. The longings of my heart to go deeper in my spirituality, beyond what I had known as spiritual practice and discipline, were shared by leaders my age all around the country. And Webber was leading us through with his leadership.

What started out as a journey to be more holistic in my worship practice led me to Webber's teaching on how to link theology, ministry, and mission. He explained that spirituality was a process of becoming human both individually and corporately, which was the exact articulation I needed in order to understand how a chosen proximity to the poor and oppressed could help believers experience the example of Christ more completely and enable us to actively participate in God's redemptive action to rescue the world.

> Through Jesus, the perfected second Adam, we see what man is called to be. The community of Jesus, the church, is called to be a corporate witness to what reconciled humanity, living as the extension of Jesus in the world, can become and will ultimately be in the kingdom of the future.
>
> True spirituality is the process of becoming human individually and corporately. This kind of spirituality, grounded in God's mission to the world, moves within the circle to action. True spirituality compels Christians to put themselves in the position of the poor and oppressed. It illuminates for believers how the exercise of Christ's ministry in the church and to the world works to liberate humanity from the demeaning effects of poverty and injustice. It releases the human spirit to participate in God's current, continuing redemptive action in history, which is moving toward God's

ultimate victory over all evil and an eternal reign over all creation. Spirituality is a link between mission, theology and ministry. It is not so much a knowing but a being—a true embodiment of God's mission.

By living in my proximate place, putting my learned theology into ministry practice, I was beginning to catch God's mission to rescue the world. As I caught this mission, it drove me to a deeper desire for theology and study, which in turn I put into practice, which caused me to further catch God's mission to rescue the world. The longer I stayed proximate, the more I practiced, engaged, and did ministry based on deepening theology, bringing me to a greater sense of God's overall mission.

We may feel a little cynical about rescuing the world, since we are taught not to love it (1 John 2:15) and we know the world is not focused on loving Jesus or his ways. This idea of agape love, where we sacrifice and don't worry about the outcome, can leave us feeling like we want to leave the world—or at least our country—and quick.

Orthodoxy, a classic in Christian apologetics written by G. K. Chesterton, speaks of our natural response toward unlovely things like our world and its brokenness. While acknowledging our natural inclination to forgo the world out of disillusionment that our efforts and sacrifice might not be worth it, Chesterton shares a perspective on engaging this explicitly broken place:

> The world . . . is the fortress of our family with the flag flying on the turret, and the more miserable it is the less we should leave it. The point is not that this world is too sad to love or too glad not to love; the point is that when you do love a thing, its gladness is a reason for loving it, and its sadness a reason for loving it more.

Loving sincerely is not for believers of small faith. The proximate environment stretches our ability to both give and receive love. Sincerely receiving love is as difficult as sincerely giving love. It is a cycle of true community in which we embrace and are embraced, where we are all broken, where we share common human bondage and the shared hope of resurrection. We may be the leaders but we are never the Comforter, the Healer, or the Savior. We are the followers of Christ, who asks us to deny ourselves, take up our cross, and follow him—to love as he loved.

While we live our lives in response to what we see in proximity, we recognize what author and speaker Jeanne Damoff articulates: "We weren't created for self-seeking comfort and ease. It lulls us to sleep. We were made to shine light in darkness, to love and serve our enemies, and to wash the feet of the least."

Loving the broken people we meet on our journey in proximity will always bring us to a point of questioning how much we have to sacrifice. The very nature of pure, sincere, sacrificial love that Jesus both demonstrated and calls us to follow is a daily process calling us deeper.

A friend and colleague who is a bivocational pastor and real estate agent was talking to me about the cost of discipleship and God's call in our lives to go deeper. She told me it felt like swimming on a good hair day. Sometimes you simply look good, and the last thing you want to do is get in a pool and go all the way in. Your friends, spouse, or kids call to you, so you say, "Okay, I'll get in, but don't splash me and don't get me wet. I like my hair today and it's not getting wet." As the sun gets hotter and your desire to go under the water is checked against your desire to keep your hair dry and looking good, you're left with a question: Will I go in all the way? Will I let my hair get wet? Will I ruin the version of me that I like right now for a deeper engagement?

God is calling us all the way in, and until we are willing to allow the cool waters of his call to mess up the way we perceive ourselves and our intentions, we are limiting our opportunity to be free. The journey exposes us and changes us so we do not come up to the surface the same as we went in. But with satisfaction we realize that we don't need or want to go back. Life is richer when we are entirely in.

Journeying On

The Lord of the Rings is a classic tale of an impossible journey. Frodo, the protagonist, is a lowly hobbit who is given a gold ring that he must bring to be melted by the flames of Mordor so that the world can continue and be in harmony. While Frodo is the most unlikely of carriers, not someone even remotely equipped to encounter the terrors and challenges of his journey, he does end the tale accomplishing what he set out to do.

I had never read the books—fantasy is not my thing—but after a long time I finally gave in to the pressure and watched the (very long) films, which I now think are fabulous. I watched them in segments; life called so often that it took some time to finish. All along I expected Frodo to die. I told my husband I thought he would fling himself into the flames of Mordor and melt along with the ring. I was shocked that he went on breathing, walking, living. The elves kept saying that the destiny would destroy him. I expected some type of dramatic death.

After destroying the ring in Mordor, Frodo returns to the Shire, his place of origin, at least for a time. At the conclusion of the movie, he shares his thoughts about the impact his journey has had on him and the reconciling of the old life he once knew.

"How do you pick up the threads of an old life?" he asks. "How do you go on when in your heart you begin to understand there is no going back? There are some things that time cannot mend, some hurts that go too deep, that have taken hold."

The fact is, journeys change the traveler. The longer the journey, the greater the change. And while it's true we cannot predict how or when the changes will occur or the outcome of the journey, we are given the opportunity to see God and his body in new ways. We are invited to follow his lead, to lean into love by turning our talk of loving and rescuing the world into redemptive action. We journey with Jesus on his mission to rescue a broken world.

Chapter Five

RACE MATTERS

*A*s a white Christian justice advocate, my skin color is a constant source of discussion and personal reflection. From the early days when I talked of proximate living in a community of color to recent days working on issues that affect a disproportionate number of black and brown people, it's been a pretty common refrain to hear: "But you aren't black" or "But you're white" is given as a reason I should not work in my proximate place.

It's true. I am white. I cannot change the color of my skin. I cannot change the background from which I came. I cannot fix the problems of the past. I cannot solve the issues of racism in the present. I am beyond limited. Yet I cannot ignore that I have a role to play, and I need to play it in a sincere way, giving deference to those people of color with whom I journey.

Racism is a reality. Whether we as white people feel responsible for it or not, we need to engage this issue if we want to love well in our life of proximity. Racism, which is defined most simply as prejudice with power, is not something we can ignore.

Well, I guess we can always ignore it, but that's a twin to doing nothing with what we know.

In this chapter I hope to lay out how a white Christian justice advocate can join people of color in their struggle against injustice. Although I recognize that not everyone in my audience is white, it is the paradigm from which I share. My hope is that there are elements in this chapter that can enlighten all of us as we journey toward justice together. I also want to hit the raw issues that those of us who enter into communities of color need to evaluate. As we walk through our own racial identity, progressing through the stages of accepting our role in community, it's good for us to be informed of a few things of which we might not be aware.

The tendency as we deepen our engagement in proximity is to think we need a formal education on everything Martin Luther King Jr. said or a degree in African American studies. Those are good things, and if you're heading that direction, great. But for those of us who were directed to study other things, this chapter will at least offer an overview and provide some direction for further investigation.

Nobody that I know moves into a proximate community of color thinking they are a racist. But I do know that white people move into communities of color hoping their skin color won't be noticed or that it doesn't matter.

After more than two decades in this world, I am here to tell you two things: they notice, and it matters. There is simply too much history to pretend there isn't a divide. Whether we like it or not, if we are white, we bring every stereotype with us into our relationships. Even when we've been around a long time, we have to build bridges again with every new relationship with a person of color.

This is something we just have to know and accept. My experience has shown that the more you practice building bridges across the racial divide, the faster it happens when you have to begin again.

Of course, people of color are not the only ones with stereotypes to overcome. In past chapters I have talked about my fear of my new community and the countless dreamers like me with stereotypes that kept them from becoming proximate, or at least staying for long. While bridges need to be built toward many different groups of people—the homeless, gang members, prostitutes, disabled people, and the list goes on—here I want to specifically talk about building bridges with people of color.

I am not an expert. I have simply had decades of opportunities to practice. I have made many mistakes and still make them—but I keep trying because I believe in a reconciled body of Christ that transforms people on both sides in the process of leaning into love. I need my brothers and sisters of color terribly, and even though there is much hurt and pain, they need me too. It is worth the struggle of admitting this issue exists because we cannot ignore the elephant in the room when it sucks out all the good air with its smelly self.

As a white person myself, I know the "Christian white person" type pretty well. In addition to thinking, hoping, and praying that they themselves aren't racist, they want to like people of color. They don't know many (if any), and they aren't typically shaped by their teaching, but they aren't against people of color. They also have not been challenged to overcome their white thinking.

When people ask me how to build bridges to people of color I tell them, of course, to become proximate—notice a theme here?—but I also tell them to begin to listen to the voices of color. Seek out their books, their sermons, their teachings. Begin to allow your intellect to be shaped by the way they see the world. Respect their instruction as leaders and sit under their teaching—not as an anomaly but as a way of life.

Several of my CCDA friends often use hashtags such as #authorsofcolor, #womenofcolor, and #speakersofcolor. These hashtags spell out a very simple message that I have interpreted as "Hear me; listen to my message; follow my leadership. I have things to contribute. Let my voice be represented." I hear them in this, and I agree that their voices are in no way beneath their more utilized and respected white male contemporaries (sorry, guys, but the white girls don't have much authority or power either—thanks for reading my book).

This makes my heart break, because as a white woman who hails from the privileged church, I know their cries are going virtually unheard. These are amazing leaders whom I have followed and continue to follow, but beyond ensuring that we as a Christian culture "represent" people of color, we have very little idea how to bridge the gap toward restoration and reconciliation.

Once again we know how to talk about it, but we don't know how to do something with what we know. That is not a good response. There is no safe road toward reconciliation. It is hard, uphill, and deeply personal for everyone. If Christ reconciled us to God and to each other, we have what we need. We need to believe this and move forward against the lies that tell us we cannot be one.

My personal journey began right before I left college. I was what Janet Helms, an acclaimed psychologist and expert on racial identity, refers to as "the happy racist." The happy racist is someone who is oblivious to issues around race. They generally feel good about themselves, feel positive about people of color, and value the fair treatment of people of all races. Helms categorizes the development of individual white identity in two stages: abandonment of racism and defining a nonracist identity. In order to engage issues of race completely, we need to come to grip with our own identity. Moving from abandonment of racism toward defining a nonracist identity is a deeply spiritual and individual work. A proximate life gives us the opportunity to practice and work through each important phase of awareness and understanding. To do this work we need to be willing to see our inherent brokenness and humbly allow ourselves to be schooled toward healing. This cannot happen outside of relationships with people of color.

I believe that the white privileged church is filled with people who are in stage one of Helms's model. They truly want to see an end to racism but are ignorant of the issues at varying levels. There are some haters, but in my experience, white church congregants recognize the past is filled with problems that need to be overcome. I believe there are two major reasons the white church does not engage in issues around racism. The first is they are simply ignorant or doubtful of the pain and divide racism still causes. Second, they are afraid to move forward because they don't know what to do or fear they'll get it wrong and their efforts will be rejected. This dilemma creates conflict, and when it does, white people either avoid people of color altogether or work to deny any personal blame for perpetuating racial injustice. Sometimes they even go so far as to deny that racism and systemic injustice toward people of color exists.

I want to tell my white friends that it's okay to be ignorant when you start to journey in nonhomogenous circles. There is room to learn. It's okay to make mistakes; there is forgiveness even for paternalistic racists. I know this because if there was ever someone who was ignorant, I was at the front of the line. I was really, really uninformed. I'd like to think the days of ignorance surrounding racism in our churches are over, but through relationships and experience, I can say with certainty that we have a lot to learn about our history.

Learning Our History

With only ten weeks left of college, I had not only come to terms with my future chosen proximity but I was excited to begin to live it out. All I had to do was finish school, and I had just three classes left. I only cared about being done, and when I learned that I needed a history class, someone told me that Social Movements was an easy A. All you did was watch movies and take essay exams—my thing! I signed up right away.

What I didn't know was what the class actually covered. Oh how thankful I am that God works with foolishness and young naiveté. This was the class that would begin to change my perspective forever and cause me to begin to pray prayers that to this day have begun to be answered. This is the class that opened my eyes to the deep pain of our country's racist history and the lack of engagement perpetuated by the privileged church—my lack of awareness was a case in point.

At the time of this class I was twenty-two. I had an apartment on reserve in Dallas that I would occupy a few short months later. I was checking my boxes to make life happen. I thought I had learned what I needed to head into this life and world, but God was about to blow my mind!

On the first day of the Social Movements class a group of us seniors sat down to watch our first film. We were all white with middle-class income security sitting in a room in southwest Ohio. The film series we began to watch was *Eyes on the Prize*. It had a catchy introductory jingle that we began to sing right away. We were cavalier and shallow. We were excited to be done with school. We all needed this education. I don't know how the class impacted the others, but I took what I learned and quietly processed.

Having grown up in proximity to African Americans, I was not prepared for what I saw in this class in 1993: clips of hoses turned on black people, the terrors of Jim Crow, the myriad injustices done to the African American community. I was shocked. I was horrified. I was appalled. I was all of these things and more, not just because they happened but because I'd had no idea!

No one had told me about the civil rights movement. I'd sat for years in Christian school and church as an excellent student—so you can't blame the fact that I wasn't paying attention—and never heard anything except the name Martin Luther King Jr. And what I knew about him was that he'd had affairs, so I shouldn't listen to him. That was the sum total of what I knew. So, so wrong!

Here I was getting ready to be married and begin a shared life that would be shaped by the African American struggle of racism, and I didn't know any of the "whys" of how it came into being.

I guess I had thought racism was an old-fashioned word for white people in the South being unable to get over the Civil War. That holds some truth but not enough of the truth.

I'm not really sure why the subject never came up. I sometimes wonder if it's because I was born so soon after the civil rights movement that society was still processing all of it. I wonder if it's because the white church was unwilling to admit any wrong-doing. I still have no idea why we would not want to teach our children about such grave injustices. I certainly learned copious amounts about Germany's Hitler and his terrorist acts on the Jewish people. Why would we not teach about terrorist acts against our own people?

Regardless of the whys, learning about the civil rights movement shut me up pretty much immediately. It wasn't that I did not want to talk about it, but it showed me how little I could trust my knowledge and experience. I had much to learn; it was time not to talk but to listen.

I had already assumed I had a lot to learn about life, especially in my new community, but this class showed me I didn't know what I had *not* learned. I had no idea what pain African Americans had endured; I needed to be a watchful student of people and their struggles. I was also sorry I hadn't known, because I couldn't care until I did.

One major reaction to this newfound knowledge was some serious anger. How could the church not speak of this great injustice? Surely the church was engaged in the battle, but I hadn't heard about this either. While much of my anger and questioning remained inside, I did begin to ask questions about the church's engagement during those years.

With every bit of information I learned, the sadness of my heart grew. I was ashamed of the church. I was ashamed of those of us who called ourselves Bible-believing Christians, who bragged of rightly dividing the Word of God and at the same time dismissed our role in liberating our black brothers and sisters.

I am still ashamed. Strong reactions to pain cause us to pray, and it was at that time that I began to pray. I prayed that if there was ever a civil rights issue in my lifetime that the church would not miss it this time. I prayed that if they once again shamelessly did ignore it, I would not. And not only would I please not miss it, but, God, would you allow me to be right in the center of it?

That's the prayer I prayed, and that's the prayer I believe set off a course of spiritual events leading me right up to where I am today. I left that moment in my history at age twenty-two—twenty-three years ago—and moved into a poor neighborhood. It was the kind I was reared to be afraid of and stay away from, riddled with the kind of crime and suffering I only watched on TV, open, oozing pain that would keep me up at night wondering if I would ever find peace in this restless place.

I was living right inside the pain of others but only one step away from the reality of my old life of optional suffering, clean places, neat lines, and solvable problems. I did long for the old and familiar but was left as someone who now knew too much to return. What was I going to do with what I knew? How could I walk away?

I knew then and still know too much to walk away. It was God's plan all along. Mine was a heart meant to know much, to mourn deeply, and to share alongside the struggle of people whose life choices are limited by structural and systemic injustice. But that does not mean that I am alone.

The Body of Christ

I have a friend who is blind in one eye. Years ago I remember him talking about how having vision in only one eye was no big deal to him because he'd never known anything different. The body is an amazing and resilient piece of equipment. It compensates for what it doesn't have even though it could run more effectively with all its working parts.

As my friend talked about his compensating eye, I began thinking. First, two eyes are better than one, and second, the body without two eyes doesn't have a complete picture of what's really going on. Don't get me wrong; I am glad my friend's body compensates. I just have two working eyes and know how awesome it is to see well.

This illustration began to make me think about the racially siloed body of Christ and the reason we need to work toward reconciliation. We are incomplete without each other. We need each voice, each unique perspective to strengthen the entire body. Unfortunately, in our churches we are so limited by comfort and familiarity that we don't even realize we aren't complete. We aren't willing to do the work to see what it would be like not to have to compensate for what we don't have.

Eyes are not the only things that compensate. If you have no legs, you'll figure out how to get around on your arms. If you have no hands, you'll learn to use your feet. Our bodies adapt to whatever circumstances we need them to, and while this is impressive in many ways, when it comes to the body of Christ, it doesn't have to be.

I personally think that as a church we are walking around with missing appendages that would be present and functional if we simply recognized that we are not complete without each other.

I see this especially in dominant-culture churches. We are so egocentric that we think we're complete the way we are. Our individualistic culture keeps us from even considering that there's something to be gained from other voices—and not just during Black History Month or Cinco de Mayo. As a body I think we compensate for what we don't have so well that we have no idea we're lacking important members (Galatians 3:28).

I am not speaking against monoethnic congregations that come together around a similar language and cultural expression. But the reality is we need to recognize and practice valuing each member of the body as a necessary contributor. The dominant culture needs to be made aware of and then become willing to follow minority culture and not be so quick to force those on the margins to adapt and conform. If we try to "melt" together, we miss out on the strength of diversity. We have so much to gain by valuing each other.

When looking at race and cultural divisions in the body of Christ, we must look through the lens of truth that God who created us equally is not a respecter of persons. God does not think people who are white, black, or brown or people who are rich or poor or somewhere in between have varying levels of value. All human beings share the same value in the kingdom of God. We see this clearly in Genesis 1, then reinforced in the New Testament (specifically in Galatians 3:28), that God values non-Jews, women, slaves, and free people all the same. We are all one in Christ.

Furthermore, we need the entire body of Christ to effectively engage God's mission to rescue the world. We are incomplete without each other.

Giving Deference

The recent Black Lives Matter narrative has left even a seasoned veteran of living in proximity to communities of color a little fearful. I am incredibly upset that we continue to stand at a racial divide and the church is still unwilling to see collective racial injustice toward people of color.

It's hard to know what to do with people's grief. It's easy for me to simply say, "Share each other's pain." But what does that look like? As I said before, I'm not an expert but I am a seasoned practitioner of reconciliation.

The death of Michael Brown and the rise of the Black Lives Matter movement was the precursor to a solid year of videos depicting the violent deaths of unarmed black men at the hands of the law enforcement community. My cousin is a cop and I know these are uncomfortable conversations, especially in the white community. But discomfort aside, it was a horrible year. A lot of the evidence pointed to a persistent problem that had been present for a long time but suddenly was in the spotlight.

One day during that time as I drove away from a meeting, I saw a group of high-school students, hands raised, walking the streets toward the capitol after leaving their classrooms in protest. I began to cry. It was not the first and would not be the last of this type of protest, but I cried that day for that group of students and the anger they felt at their reality. I have a front view to this situation and it's simply painful to see.

It was early December after advent had begun and the following Sunday would be the week of "peace" in the liturgical calendar. The image of the angry students joining the collective anger across the country was ringing in my ears. How could we work together to engage this crisis again? How could we lean into the collective pain? How could we publicly suffer together?

I had heard that friends and leaders of churches in Chicago were organizing a walkout during their services that Sunday. They were going to hit the streets with their hands in the air—"Hands up; don't shoot!"—and lie on the ground with shirts and signs that stated, "Black Lives Matter" and "I Can't Breathe." I wanted to do it in Denver.

I texted a few friends that Friday morning and asked them if they would join the Chicago group's walkout. We called in all the favors we could with churches in the city, and about half of them agreed to take part—not as a walkout but as a peace march. Most of the churches that agreed were multicultural city churches. Some churches were excited to add to the narrative, some were skeptical, and some were resistant, but we moved forward with what we believed we needed to do.

After the texts began to fly, I went over to my friend's office at Open Door to talk about the idea. She was reserved but open. As a well-respected African American leader, she knew that engagement was important, but would the church's involvement be sincere?

I saw in her eyes her hesitation to tell me how she felt when I lamented what was happening in our country against African Americans. We were friends. We had talked of a variety of issues in the past, working closely together, but the pain of systemic racism was rearing its ugly head, causing us all to go back to our corners and figure out who we could trust.

I sensed her hesitancy to share her pain. So, knowing my white skin represented racial injustice, tyranny, oppression, hate, and justified murder, I invited her to yell at me. We went back and forth as she worked courageously to get out every sentence.

"What do you people want?" she whispered. I implored her to keep going.

"What do you people want from us?" The pain and anger in her voice grew louder and became more real. I could handle it. We are wrong. You are hurt. I care about your pain. Take it out on me. I am safe. You can trust me not to hurt you or deny your reality.

The back-and-forth went on for a while until we ended in a heap on her floor, crying and weeping for the pain and violence against people of color by people who looked like me. The raw emotion of our inability to fix the problem in that moment and our willingness to share a sacred space of hurt, anger, and committed love for sisters was what we took to the march that Sunday.

We did not get the turnout we had hoped for, but one never does, especially with two days' lead time. About three hundred people met us and walked together along Colfax, first in conversation and then in silence. We carried purple candles of advent to represent peace. Peace in our country, yes, but a bigger peace as well. Peace that only the Prince of Peace can bring with his radical shalom, which leaves nothing broken and everything restored.

My friend and I walked to the steps of the capitol that day praying and weeping alongside each other as sisters. I listened to her cries and shared my tears, listened to her pain and shared it. I am a mother of sons but they are not black. She has reason to be afraid for her boys' very lives.

I cannot overstate the importance of walking alongside—not in front of or behind—those people who are directly impacted by pain. Sure, in proximity you will have experiences driven by racial bias both implicit and explicit, but it is not the same as being a direct target of racism. Sure, I have some hurts and even some scars, but I was not born into them. We hail from a long line of privileged human beings who at some point began to name who was and was not valuable, bringing us to this place—a siloed church separated by fear and the lie that we cannot be one.

If we want to see racial discrimination become obsolete, the church needs to first of all admit that racism is not an individual issue but a societal issue that affects our brothers and sisters in tragic ways. We cannot sit on the sidelines with the hope that things will change. We must actively engage in seeking the betterment of people's lives.

Moving Forward

Understanding that people of color have deep pain and need solidarity can still leave us wondering what to do or how to do it in a way that doesn't add to their pain. My suggestion is to simply ask.

Living in proximity means we are rooted in relationship, so we can ask. We don't have to be scared. People will be honest if we have built up enough trust. We must be humble, not cavalier. We are not seeking facts; we are trying to be a good friend. I am still learning this, and since the playing field is dynamic and always evolving, I still ask and try not to assume too much as things change.

Not that long ago I was sitting with a small group of friends having breakfast. My friend was wearing yet another #BlackLivesMatter T-shirt. This was his regular attire, and even though I wasn't a big T-shirt wearer, I wanted one. But I wondered if that would be seen as problematic since I'm white. I wanted to ask if it was okay, and then I worried that as a seasoned leader working alongside a reconciliation movement I should already know the answer.

With fear and reservation, I asked, "Is it okay for a white woman like me to wear a Black Lives Matter T-shirt?"

I will never forget the kindness in my friends' eyes and voices as they said yes. They could hear the fear in my voice, I am sure, which is probably why they were so gentle. But then I explained why I was so uncertain.

The night before I had received a phone call from my daughter whose college classmates were protesting a dean whose office had dressed up in Mexican mariachi attire for Halloween and put it on social media.

My daughter was upset. She understood why this stunt was offensive, but her new white friends at the college were saying that "once again minorities are making a big deal out of nothing." She was upset at them, of course, but she was also outside her established place in a community of color, and her own racial identity was less secure. People of color were angry, and while she shared their anger and even marched behind the evening's Black Lives Matter protest, she began to understand what it was like to be white. Up until college she was typically the only white person in her peer group—a safe place since the minority culture in that moment does not feel threatened by just one person.

She was trying to explain to her minority friends at college that up until this moment, the white students had never perceived themselves as racist or insensitive. The progressive nature of the school they'd chosen had freed them from thinking of themselves as a part of the problem. Those were the "other" kind of white people.

In that moment my daughter, reared as a dominant-culture minority in a Latino neighborhood, was white. And she was learning firsthand what everyone who is white has to learn at some point—that all white people are implicated in our country's history of racism.

As a white person you may feel this isn't fair. Maybe not. But it's also not fair to be born into a system that explicitly undervalues your body, your perspective, and your very presence in American culture because of the color of your skin.

Step one is to recognize that we cannot fully understand the pain of racism. Step two is to offer our support with open arms and a posture that asks, "What would you have me do?"

Sharing the Pain of Others

In my early years of proximity I worked to develop true relationships built on equity and love with people of color in my community. As is the case with lots of bridge building, this initially was centered around food, music, and language. The easy stuff. The fun stuff. The things that keep you enjoying diversity without having to engage the pain.

These are ways that everyone—even those not following Jesus—begin to build bridges to each other. It's the easiest place to start. Eat each other's food, listen to each other's music, and learn to understand each other's cultural phrases and expressions. Although these may be the easiest places to start, they are also incredibly important. In doing this we learn to respect and value others and the way they engage and celebrate life. Experiencing the beauty of other cultures and sharing this form of hospitality together enables a deeper understanding of one another.

However, in order to share true relationships, we have to begin to embrace each other's pain. We cannot stop with shallow experiences; even the world recognizes the value of engaging that limited aspect of diversity. It's great to enjoy beans and avocados with my neighbors, but is that really building a lasting bridge of reconciliation? It's an important first step, where trust begins and then becomes tested, but it's not the end.

The news gives us no lack of rhetoric to buttress racial tendencies, whether it's videos of unarmed black men getting shot by police or nasty anti-immigrant comments made by public figures. In those moments our commitment to seeking reconciliation is tested.

When I speak of reconciliation, make no mistake—I'm not talking about representation. Minority representation on our church staffs, in our institutions, and in society is not reconciliation. Posing for selfies with African Americans and posting them on Facebook does not exempt us from the reconciliation journey that we must share individually and collectively. We as Christ-followers need to move beyond representation and its limited effort.

To be reconciled is to bear one another's pain and burdens and make them our own. To be reconciled is to courageously and boldly say that "Black Lives Matter" and "Brown Lives Matter." This theological statement, rooted in the *imago Dei*, declares that all people are divinely endowed with the image of God.

Over the course of our nation's history we have deemed black life as criminal, inferior, and subhuman. I believe that in stating "Black Lives Matter," we declare that those who have historically been rendered "the least of these" are valuable and significant, both to us and to God.

As a person of privilege whose perspective has been radically changed because of my proximity to people of color, I implore the church to continue to lean into true agape love. We as Christians *know* what love is: Jesus Christ laid down his life for us, and we ought to lay down our lives for our brothers and sisters. We must love with action and truth (1 John 3:16-18).

We also cannot elect to engage with those impacted by racial bigotry only when we can relate on some level, such as when hate makes its way into the church and kills people gathered for prayer. We also need to respond when an African American mother's son wearing a hoodie is shot and killed by a civilian, when a father must grieve the death of his son whose crime was music considered "too loud," when an unarmed black man is shot in the back while running from where he was pulled over for a traffic stop, and when a man is choked to death, whispering, "I can't breathe."

When the waters are still muddied and we may not know all the details, what will the church do? What will those of us in a proximate place do? What will we do when we cannot understand our present reality and the chasm of grave injustice that separates death and life?

Above all, love each other deeply, because love covers over a multitude of sins. (1 Peter 4:8)

Whether you or I personally feel responsible for our country and the American church's racist legacy, we must recognize and own the sins that go back generations, to where humanity and privilege began to name what was valuable, bringing us to this place—a place driven by fear and separation.

Perfect love drives out fear. (1 John 4:18)

Let us not move into tomorrow with the same guarded, complicit, fearful response to the pain of the body of Christ. Instead let us take this moment to commit to lean into our collective tomorrows with sacrificial love that will build bridges to the pain of those who are hurting. It is not noble to stay on the sidelines. It is not noble to remain silent.

Greater love has no one than this: to lay down one's life for one's friends. (John 15:13)

Entering into the pain of injustice toward those with whom we are in proximity requires not only that we recognize our complicity in the pain of racism but also that we refuse to sit idly by while we witness further oppression. We must embrace the pain of people of color, follow their leadership, give deference to their experience, and join them in their fight for liberation.

Cesar Chavez, an American justice activist who led civil rights campaigns for migrant farm workers in California, understood the sacred journey alongside the voiceless. As a Mexican American who was taught the importance of education, he worked hard to become educated and gain options for his future. Recognizing that there was great need to enter into the pain of those who did not share his opportunities and access, he followed the example of Gandhi and St. Francis, joining their struggles. He articulated his heart for their pain in the following prayer:

> Show me the suffering of the most miserable;
> So I will know my people's plight.
>
> Free me to pray for others;
> For you are present in every person.
>
> Help me take responsibility for my own life;
> So that I can be free at last.
>
> Grant me courage to serve others;
> For in service there is true life.
>
> Give me honesty and patience;
> So that I can work with other workers.
>
> Bring forth song and celebration;
> So that his Spirit will be alive among us.
>
> Let the Spirit flourish and grow;
> So that we will never tire of the struggle.

Let us remember those who have died for justice;
For they have given us life.

Help us love even those who hate us;
So we can change the world.

Amen.

Chapter Six

PRIVILEGE NEEDS TO TAKE A SIDE

*L*iving in a poor community means limited access to good schools. Everyone wants their children to have opportunities to learn, grow, excel, and have a future. Therefore access to good schools is important for all children, not just those born into middle- or upper-income families.

When my oldest was preschool age, our desire for her to go to a good school was no different from my neighbors'. Living in a predominantly Spanish-speaking community, we also wanted our kids to learn to speak, read, and write Spanish—not because it was "cool" to learn another language but because it was a necessary survival skill.

You cannot imagine my delight when the first-ever public, dual-language Montessori school was proposed to the Denver school board. It was to be located a few miles from our house and would open the year our oldest began kindergarten! It was a terrific opportunity for our family and others in our community.

After the school had been open for two years, an amendment to the state's constitution was placed on the ballot proposing an English-only learning approach for ESL kids. While this probably sounded good to those who were disconnected from English language learners, in essence the bill would close our awesome community-supported school. We were upset!

We channeled our frustration toward support for what became known as the "No on 31" campaign. I was grateful for the savvy parents in our city who helped craft an effort to push back on the proposed amendment. Simply following suit, I wrote "No on 31" in shoe polish on my minivan and drove it around proudly. One Saturday there was a rally and a march. David was working, so with three kids in tow, baby in a stroller and all, we marched, chanting, "No on treinta y uno; no on 31." Reporters followed our large group snapping pictures and recording video. I had never done anything like this in my life.

After the event some friends of mine from Pueblo (a city about three hours from Denver) told me they had seen me on the front page of their local paper. There I was with my six- and four-year-old and my baby in a stroller on the front page of the paper, sign held high, fighting a state amendment. What was I doing on that front page? People from all over the state were there marching. Why did they photograph me?

I did not know then what I know now. A young white family with children was walking boldly and with conviction for an amendment that would benefit immigrant families. I was unexpected to the story. I did not fit. I had caught the attention of the media and it was telling an important and underrepresented part of the story—that white people, even those with little kids, care about immigrants' educational opportunities.

Those months working on that campaign did not feel like a campaign. It was simply not an option not to participate. Our community had done much to craft a school that met the needs of the community, and to see it come to an end because of a proposed amendment funded by someone living in California—well, we would not allow it to happen. We fought for our school.

As election day got closer I visited a friend and her husband. The husband did not agree with my take on the amendment and was debating with me. After we were done, my friend and I walked out to my van (remember all the shoe polish?) and she said something I had never considered before in my life.

"Michelle, I never realized how political you were."

"I am not political," I quickly responded, as though that were an ignoble accusation. She looked at me with a raised eyebrow and said nothing else.

I left that interaction wrestling. Was I political? No, I was simply taking part in something important. It was what our school and community badly needed. Why would I be considered political? Maybe she was right. Was that bad? How did I get to this place?

Proximity compels a response. Its transformative lens turns what we see and begin to understand into action. The action may not even be something we consider a choice because we are so intimately connected with those affected. We share their pain and are compelled to do something with what we have.

What Are You Going to Do with What You Have?

Regardless of our ethnic identity, if our proximity to the poor is a choice, we are privileged. Mine was a choice, and I am privileged to have the resources available to move in and out of my proximate place. We began this second section of the book in chapter four with a question—what are you going to do with what you know? We are going to end this section and chapter six with another question—what are you going to do with what you have? Both are key questions as we move from awareness into action against injustice.

But before we can go much further, we need to look at what privilege is and why privilege should begin to take a side.

When I refer to "privilege," I'm not talking exclusively about white privilege, although because I am white this is something I know more intimately. Being white automatically enables one to have advantages and opportunities that black or brown people do not. But when I talk about privilege in this chapter, I mean people using opportunity and influence to support issues or ideas that might not directly impact them.

Privilege is something we have when we are able to elect in and out of a chosen position. In looking at the biblical narrative, we see numerous times when God brought people into positions of privilege for the purpose of using their privilege to influence the issues of the day.

Joseph, who was unjustly brought to Egypt and imprisoned, was eventually elevated to a place of privilege in order to help save his people from starvation during famine. Moses, reared in Pharaoh's palace and familiar with the Egyptian language and cultural norms, was able to speak up on behalf of the Hebrew people and lead them out of slavery and oppression. Nehemiah, credited for rebuilding Jerusalem, would not have been able to make a successful step forward if he hadn't had a relationship with the king, who noticed in Nehemiah 2:2 he "looked sad" and gave him resources and permission to do the work.

All through the Bible we see people use their positions of leadership and privilege to speak truth to power. Privilege is not something we as Christians are given to hold and enjoy for our own benefit. Privilege and its opportunities are to be shared with those who do not have it so they can also experience fairness and equity.

Sometimes God uses people who were born into privilege. Sometimes he raises them up. King David started out as a no-name shepherd in a very small tribe in Israel, and his own family forgot to call him in to the big ceremony with Samuel. Yet God chose to bring him to power so that God's kingdom could be advanced through his lineage. Christ, David's great-great-great-[and so on]-grandson, fulfilled the ultimate plan of redemption.

Why Are You Here?

Years ago I began to realize that God didn't bring me to my proximate place so that I could simply have information for my own well-being or set up a new life for myself alongside a new community. Instead I needed to help bridge two divides so we could make change together. I am committed to the reconciliation of the church, and that is the work I need to remain committed to as a person of privilege living life in proximity to the poor.

While my understanding of issues such as racism and disdain for the poor eventually became more clear, I found them hard to name initially. Comments made by individuals were easy to see and call out. However, it was challenging to explain what I was coming to understand. Defining racism specifically was like trying to hit a moving target.

I have ultimately come to understand that racism, while hard to name individually except in overt expressions, is easy to see collectively in systems. Racism, oppression, exclusion—all of the brokenness under the auspices of injustice—manifests itself in systems. These systems need to be called out and changed. Those who are impacted by broken systems benefit greatly when people with privilege join them in their struggle. People of privilege need to be willing to join people trapped by those systems to help build a bridge toward a greater movement of change. We need to be willing to restore what is broken, moving past our private convictions to occupy a public place and help make change.

We see from the prophet Isaiah that lip service to God is not enough. The people of God cannot simply go through the motions of following God in prayer, sacrifices, and fasting but instead must worship him both individually and collectively through action. Isaiah describes how tired God is of acts of worship that do not lead to internal and external change. He calls God's people to

> Wash yourselves, make yourselves clean;
> Put away the evil of your doings from before My eyes.
> Cease to do evil,
> Learn to do good;
> Seek justice,
> Rebuke the oppressor;
> Defend the fatherless,
> Plead for the widow. (Isaiah 1:16-17 NKJV)

The call to "rebuke the oppressor" states the need to actively restore what is broken. When we are in proximity to the poor it is easier to see what is broken, name it, and move to help restore it. It requires that we side with the poor and stand against those who either benefit from keeping the brokenness in place or do not understand that it's even broken.

I have relationships with the poor. I am deeply aware of their struggles. I am so familiar with their issues that I have no problem whatsoever standing on their side or advocating alongside them or on their behalf. But that was not always the case. Even after my illumination, it took courage to begin to publicly call out what I was seeing.

Immigration is an area where I began to speak more publicly in a definitive way. Immigration is a political hot button that impacts a national audience, which is code for "everyone has an opinion." At the time of my turning point in this area, there was not a lot of awareness around the injustice of immigration beyond certain communities. Yet tensions were growing.

Living alongside immigrants and sharing their struggles brought me to a place of choosing their side. My first time speaking to a public audience about my personal convictions regarding immigration and my faith, I was the opening speaker for a rally calling on people to recognize that pro-life meant pro-immigrant. It may seem obvious now, but then it was a politically toxic issue, and the church had very little understanding of the issue beyond what they heard from politicians. Those of us who worked in immigrant communities and raised money from the privileged church were beginning to tread into a territory that was fast becoming hostile.

I remember walking up to the microphone very nervous. I knew what I wanted to share and I had the passion and conviction to boot, but the words would bring me to a public place that I could not pull back from. I started my speech that day with this statement: "I am an evangelical Christian and I care about immigrants." To share that I wasn't just a Christian but "evangelical" was risky for a number of reasons. The word was associated with conservative politics and an anti-immigrant narrative at the time, and it was hard to admit that association to those in my proximate urban place. People hadn't realized that I was from that particular Christian camp, and classifying myself was difficult. My declaration of love for immigrants and willingness to speak against the injustice they faced caused the people in my community of origin to react in negative ways. I personally could not win. Yet immigrants could.

My place of insight compelled and still compels me to take sides on immigration and a host of issues that impact the poor and oppressed. People in my former life, who have conservative leanings and often look at these systemic issues as merely political, get frustrated beyond belief that I am pushing back against the status quo.

Because of my proximity to the poor and because of my former life of privilege I am on a constant bridge, yet that does not mean I am in the middle. Being a bridge is not being in the middle.

I do not believe that staying in the middle of a justice issue to "keep both sides happy" is noble. Standing in the middle may help you feel like you can hear both sides, but in reality it breathes life into the lie that injustice does not exist and that oppression does not need to be rebuked. There are not two sides to justice. People of privilege who refrain from choosing the side of the poor demonstrate their privilege over and over again. Only from a distance do we think fixing oppression and injustice is someone else's job. That is why proximity is powerful. Proximity compels us to choose a side.

Engaging the pain of another's struggle is not some noble decision but a natural result of sincere relationships. Valuing people enables us to see that we cannot shrink back from love that manifests itself through standing alongside them in their need to be fully restored.

When those of us who are privileged side with the poor, *then* we are able to build a bridge back to where we came from and help others join the poor in their struggle. This helps liberate us all from injustice. This is how we confront systems of racism and oppression. When we see its manifestation in systems and are willing to call it out publicly, we can be a part of working together toward restoration.

Justice Is Above the Law

But what about obeying and following the law? I regularly hear people talk about the 11.5 million undocumented people in our country as "illegals" who need to be deported and Romans 13:1 is cited in support—we don't have to look any more deeply into the issue because those "illegals" broke the law. We think of laws as the top of the food chain and those who don't fit within the parameters of the law just need to get with the program and do what is right. And as Christians, it's our job to make sure they do it, right?

Not so fast.

I am not calling for disobedience to the law, but I do maintain that human laws are not supreme. Even godly human laws are not supreme. God's heart and his justice are to guide our thoughts and actions, and we as Christians should not be so quick to defend a system we do not completely understand. We need to recognize that God calls for justice, and justice is above rules and laws.

A few years ago I was giving an immigration presentation. The audience was made up of pastors from Idaho who were nearly all white and male, and they were conservative in their politics. As I spoke, I could see that one gentleman looked unsettled. From the beginning I honed in on him and tried to be my kindest, gentlest, most persuasive self without getting too soft or off track. His face didn't budge. I remember thinking, "Well, Michelle, you can't win them all."

After I finished, as I talked up front with people who were mostly excited and eager, he stayed back by himself but positioned himself in a way that looked like he was waiting to speak with me. I had no intention of backing out of this potentially difficult conversation, but I certainly was going to make him wait. For one, I wanted him to continue to calm down if he was ready to tell me off, and two, I didn't want to make anyone else standing around feel uncomfortable or have them shift in their support of the day's conversation as a result of our pending conversation.

I finally turned toward him and asked if he wanted to talk about something. He opened with this question: "So what you are saying is that you're above the law?"

These are the kinds of questions that make one panic inside, get a little defensive, and even deny whatever it is you said to invoke such an outrageous accusation. My mind began to race. *What did I say? How do I get out of this one? How mad is he at me?* All of these questions raced through my mind as I gathered my words for a response.

"I'm not sure I understand exactly what you mean by 'above the law.' Can you explain a little more?"

He tried to explain. As I listened intently he talked about moral decisions, justice, law, ethics, and a class he had taken in college more than thirty years earlier. I realized he was recalling Lawrence Kohlberg's stages of moral development.

Kohlberg was a well-respected professor and psychologist who categorized ethical behavior in six developmental stages categorized under three headings: pre-conventional morality, conventional morality, and post-conventional morality. In essence these stages help define how a person makes decisions around right and wrong.

Stage one, or pre-conventional morality, asks questions like, "What will happen to me if I do this? Will I be punished or rewarded for this?" These are the most primal reasons we make decisions around right or wrong. Animals and toddlers make choices based on this low-level reasoning guided by negative and positive consequences.

In stage two, or conventional morality, we conform to societal norms, laws, and rules. We see this in young children when they begin to realize they aren't the only people in the world and begin to make choices that are socially appropriate. At some point in our socialization we stopped screaming and throwing ourselves on the floor to show our disapproval; we realized that no one else our age was using that approach. We follow rules because they are the rules or because they are so obviously a part of society that rules don't even need to be set. Chew with your mouth closed. Don't scream out in the middle of someone's stage performance. Don't run red lights. Pay your taxes. It's the rule whether it's written or understood. Don't ask questions—just do what you're told.

As we move up the stages of making moral decisions based on right and wrong, we begin to realize that exceptions to the rule can exist. We realize that some rules are outdated and some should never have been created in the first place. There needs to be a space to alter the rules, which moves us to the third stage: post-conventional morality.

This third and final stage contains two levels: social contract orientation and universal ethical principles. Social contract orientation supports the following of an existing rule with the understanding that if the rule needs to be changed, there is opportunity to do that. This is the essence of our democracy. We have laws. If the law works for the common good it should be upheld; if not, it should be changed. We as Americans love that our laws are contract-based with the freedom to change them by majority votes. But we also have three branches of government and a checks-and-balances system to ensure we aren't whimsical in our rule changing.

Universal ethical principal is the highest of Kohlberg's stages. This stage goes beyond specific laws and speaks of a universal code of ethical engagement that at some time might cause us to break an established law.

As I was growing up I heard stories of missionaries smuggling Bibles across borders into Russia with no regard for Russian law. In fact, they looked for ways to actively break the law so that people in that country could have access to the Bible. There are also stories of Corrie ten Boom's Dutch family breaking the law by hiding Jews from the Nazis (see tenboom.org), Dietrich Bonhoeffer trying to overthrow and assassinate Hitler (dbonhoeffer.org), and even the mother of Moses hiding her baby in her home for three months instead of allowing him to be killed. These are just a few examples of people who did not allow the law of a land to dictate how they responded to an unjust law.

When I was sharing about our broken immigration system up in Idaho, debunking the common misconceptions perpetuated in the media, the pastor I thought was angry was simply thinking deeply. He was beginning to realize that this "system" he had perceived as good and right harbored some disturbing injustices, and that while obeying the law is good (second level of Kohlberg's stages), the ability to provide for one's family, keep a family of mixed immigration status together, or flee gang threats goes beyond simple law—it speaks to ethical principles of justice.

It was as though the light bulb went off for both of us in that moment. "Yes," I eagerly answered. "Justice is above the law!"

Oh, the relief and the enthusiasm with which we eagerly interacted. We began to talk of Bonhoeffer and ten Boom. We discussed how human law does not always imply justice but that justice is defined by God's Word—and how we as his church should obey God's justice above all. That experience was significant since it enabled me to more strongly articulate our responsibility to stand for justice even above existing law, and to recognize that all humanity—especially the church—is called to a higher form of engagement.

This is often where I find myself rubbing up against the Christian leaders with whom I interact. How far do we engage justice? Do we hear of an injustice and refuse to take action, thinking the law creating the injustice needs to remain simply because it's the law? Is the law good and worth upholding—or does it need to change?

Changing the Law

Years ago when I was developing my own understanding of justice and its relation to the existing law, I heard a story told by a pastor speaking at a CCDA conference.

A church group went into a courthouse to stand alongside some friends whose slumlord was exposing them to horrid conditions in their apartment complex. They had convincing evidence and presented it clearly to the judge. The slumlord was taking advantage of his tenants without remorse. But when it came time for the judge to rule, he sided with the slumlord.

The group erupted in emotion. The pastor cried out, "Judge, how can you side with this slumlord? Where is the justice?"

The judge replied, "Pastor, you may be correct in your assessment of the injustice toward the tenants. But this is not a court of justice; rather, it is a court of law. If you think the law is unjust, change it."

And that is when a lot of lights turned on for me. I grew up in a privileged world where the law served me well. I thought courts were institutions of justice and that everyone, if given their proper day in court, would get the justice they deserved. That is not the case, and I know and believe it with conviction because I have witnessed it at very deep levels. Proximity to injustice and the limitations of poverty and marginalization teach this repeated chorus over and over again. Just because something is a law does not mean it serves the cause of justice. We need to enable the courts of law to rule in a manner that brings about justice for all people.

There is no waiting on this. Things don't just slowly and consistently work themselves out. We need to actively speak against injustice. We should not ask people to wait for justice to find them. If the laws don't work for them, they cannot trust the system. The laws must be changed, and they need the voice of the privileged to join them.

I want to take some time to remind us of our history. It's easy to look at times in our past when leaders have used their platforms to stand alongside oppression, and history cheers their noble decisions. We often think that we would be those leaders today if faced with similar issues of injustice.

The reality is that in the midst of polarizing issues that call for the privileged to step up and take sides, our willingness to do so is challenged by rejection and backlash from people in our previous communities. It is hard to lead in the face of opposition (and I will discuss those natural fears in an upcoming section), but it is imperative that we move forward and not shrink back from taking direct action to help create change.

Two leaders in the Gospels could have had nice, privileged lives of respect if they had gone along with the status quo, but instead they were agents of the gospel, and its justice compelled them to take a side against leaders both inside and outside the religious system.

Jesus was a Jew, but he was a unique Jew. He spoke with such wisdom, truth, and grace that the leaders marveled at him as a young boy. When he went to the temple with his parents, the religious leaders there were amazed at his understanding. He was recognized in the center of Judaism as an outstanding young emerging leader. And I am fairly certain that as he got older, people remembered him, talked of him, and continued to watch him. He was someone to be taken seriously. I imagine the religious leaders thought about how great it would be to have him on their leadership team.

Then he began to challenge them. As he got older and entered his life of ministry, he pointed out with more and more authority that the heart of God was being forgotten and turned into lies. The temple, he said, had become a house of thieves. Jesus chose to speak up and not side with those in power but instead hold them accountable for their lies (see Luke 19:46).

The religious leaders were oppressing the very people they were supposed to serve and teach God's heart. Jesus told the Jewish people to practice and obey whatever those leaders told them, but not to follow their example: "For they do not practice what they teach. They tie up heavy, cumbersome loads and put them on other people's shoulders, but they themselves are not willing to lift a finger to move them" (Matthew 23:3-5).

I don't want to go into all the injustices of the Pharisees, although there are many; I just want to say they knew who Jesus was and had thought he was a part of their system. They had marveled at his insight and wisdom and watched him grow. And because of that, they could not dismiss him.

Jesus was one of them in that he was a religious leader and knew what needed to be called out. Yes, he was the Son of God, but before he revealed that, he was a Jew who was not able to be disregarded. This is an important element of what I am trying to convey. Privileged people will listen to privileged people. You have a voice. When you speak and lead, even if others do not agree with you, it is hard for them to discount what you say. You are one of them, and the language they speak, the customs that are acceptable to them, are all a part of who you are. You can help connect them to the realities of your proximate place.

I have often heard—and said myself—how important it is to listen to indigenous leadership when working in a crosscultural context. One day as I was thinking through my place in the body I realized that I am indigenous too, just not to the poor. I am indigenous to the privileged church and middle-class society. My leadership alongside those who are directly impacted is a resource both to share and utilize.

The apostle Paul was not only a Jew but a Roman citizen, and because of this privilege he was afforded rights, voice, and opportunity that many leaders in the early church did not have. Paul's actions and opinions were not appreciated in many Jewish and Roman circles. He was not breaking the laws of either group, but he still made a lot of people angry. He kept picking a side and boldly professing what he believed. Because of his privilege, education, and heritage, he was well-versed in how to be both Jewish and Roman, and he used those positions to speak up for what he believed was right. He suffered greatly, but his voice was not one to disregard. He knew his rights and his message, and he even appealed his case all the way to Caesar (see Acts 25:9-12).

In addition to biblical history, I'd like to look at some American history. This segment of history shows a missed opportunity by the privileged church in regard to racism and its ugly past. The civil rights movement was focused on oppressive laws that overtly discriminated against African Americans in the South. But that was just part of the story. The rest of the story—the disgraceful part—is that the church, the privileged church, did not join the black church of the day and use its privilege to help bring about restoration. It did not use its platform anywhere, the North included, to push back in a way that would rebuke oppression. Instead, we learn from Martin Luther King Jr. that it did just the opposite.

In 1963 eight white Alabama pastors sent an open letter to Alabamans titled "Call to Unity." At that time racism had reached a fever pitch in the South. African Americans were pushing back against unjust Jim Crow laws and fighting for their right to live a fully free and integrated life. Church people in the South were beginning to question the racist status quo just slightly.

In an effort to quell some of the unrest in congregations, these eight pastors penned their letter in an effort to restore "order" by discrediting the work of Martin Luther King Jr. and those who worked with him. The privileged pastors urged people not to get riled up and join the civil rights movement but allow the legal system in place to do the job of advancing justice. They even referred to King as an outsider and labeled his efforts "unwise and untimely," working to steer people even further away from King's nonviolent protests.

This call initiated a response from King himself, an open letter written while he was jailed in Birmingham. King penned the powerful "Letter from a Birmingham Jail" in response to the lack of support he saw in what I refer to as "the privileged church." People who were not targets of oppression or peril not only sat quietly on the sidelines but actively and publicly spoke against the efforts of the minority church.

I think "Call to Unity" and "Letter from a Birmingham Jail" together show the deep contrast between the privileged and unprivileged church. "Call" was written by people who were not directly impacted by the issue at hand nor were they proximate in a way that would impart a sense of urgency or help them understand that the laws and courts were stacked against those protesting. Those of us who have not suffered injustice in an established system may not understand how there could ever be an unjust law on the books, so we label those pushing back as liberals and dismiss their efforts. An equal tragedy is when we see the injustice but for fear of backlash choose to stay on the sidelines silently.

King's "Letter" is a much more eloquent explanation of what I am trying to communicate. My strongest suggestion is that you take the time to read it. In it you can see the history of the church when it stayed silent and complicit.

What's more, the civil rights movement has not come and gone. Even now, people live in oppression and with injustice, and if we stay silent and think we are nobly standing in the middle, we reinforce what King so aptly stated years ago: "Shallow understanding from people of good will is more frustrating than absolute misunderstanding from people of ill will."

Proximity is powerful because we are unable to claim absolute misunderstanding. We are present to the pain of those in oppression. We must be willing to speak up and out. Or else we too "will have to repent in this generation not merely for the hateful words and actions of the bad people but for the appalling silence of the good people."

Neutrality with Injustice Is Not Noble

Recently the world mourned the loss of well-known and respected Holocaust survivor Elie Wiesel. Wiesel was a prisoner in both Auschwitz and Buchenwald concentration camps during the Nazi regime. Although he wrote many books, *Night*, a deeply personal account of Wiesel's time in the camps, was his most recognized. It was translated into thirty languages, bringing awareness to the world. Because of his outstanding humanitarian work in his reflections on violence, repression, and racism, Wiesel was awarded the Nobel Peace Prize in 1986.

Wiesel witnessed and experienced some of the gravest atrocities carried out in humanity's history. The suffering of the Jewish people during the Nazis' power was unparalleled; six million Jews lost their lives in this brutal display of hatred. All the while, non-Jewish people around the world worked to go about their daily lives and avoid becoming more informed lest they have to respond in action. Those who did respond are the known or unknown heroes of that time in history. Choosing to stand with the oppressed was the just thing to do.

Wiesel, who was directly impacted, recognized the importance of using his survival as an opportunity to stand boldly against what had happened. In an interview with *The New York Times* in 1981 he stated, "If I survived, it must be for some reason. In my place, someone else could have been saved. And so I speak for that person. On the other hand, I know I cannot."

Another young Jewish teen taken from her home centuries before Wiesel would be taken from his, Esther was brought to a place of prominence and privilege so that her voice could be used. This voice was not for her personal protection or affluence but to prevent the annihilation of her people by going before her husband, the king of Persia, on their behalf. This historical account demonstrates how we too, who are in a privileged place, can use our position to speak up on behalf of those who are suffering. Our privilege, like Esther's, is to be used "for such a time as this."

It is hard to choose to side with the poor and voiceless when we have to stand against privilege. Standing against privilege carries the ultimate risk of burning the bridge that leads back home. While that may happen, it should never be a motivator to stay silent or in the middle road of injustice.

We may be tempted to think that staying neutral is a better choice and try not to learn more so we can stay at least a little removed. We may justify it further by thinking it better to stay out of the view of criticism, especially the criticism of those in our communities of origin whose views have not been transformed. However, I beg you to reconsider. Those who choose to do nothing with their voice or privilege perpetuate the attitude of the Levite and the priest walking the Jericho road: aware of the pain but unwilling to go to the other side of the road, see what is happening more clearly, and get their hands dirty.

Wiesel worked tirelessly to speak up whenever people had to endure suffering and humiliation. In his Nobel Prize acceptance speech, he explained why people should not be neutral:

> Neutrality helps the oppressor, never the victim. Silence encourages the tormentor, never the tormented. Sometimes we must interfere. When human lives are endangered, when human dignity is in jeopardy, national borders and sensitivities become irrelevant.... Wherever men or women are persecuted because of their race, religion, political views, that place must—at that moment—become the center of the universe.

We as Christians cannot love our neighbors as ourselves by avoiding the journey to painful places. When we do choose to walk it, we cannot stay on the other side; at that moment, it must "become the center of [our] universe."

Privilege is a resource we bring to our proximity to the poor and its pain and injustice. As we remain proximate, gaining clarity on what is happening, moving that deep awareness to action, we will be compelled to respond in a way that pushes back on privilege.

Not long ago I was talking to a colleague about how I began this justice journey as a person of integrity and reputation and hoped that when I finished, those two things would still be in place. My brother in Christ harshly questioned my comment.

"Why should you get to leave your work with integrity and a good reputation? Jesus didn't."

Talk about hard truth. I am certainly not condoning a life characterized by lack of integrity and a bad reputation, and neither was he. But the truth is that Jesus Christ himself became proximate to humanity in a humble posture and died a perceived criminal. Who am I to think that I get to protect what he had to abandon?

Action requires prophetic, challenging truth that may cause people to question who we are. I remember talking to a friend when our ministries began to lose funding after we actively spoke against injustice. "They don't burn, stone, or kill the prophets of today, they just cut off their funding," we agreed.

And with that realization, dear justice seekers who are proximate to pain that compels a response, take courage—use what you have learned to side with the poor and oppressed. Proximity is powerful because it compels you to act in sincere ways, and what you lose in funding and approval from the privileged you gain in sustenance for the long haul.

Part Three

PROXIMITY FOR THE LONG HAUL

Chapter Seven

FEAR, COURAGE, REDEMPTION

*A*s we begin our final section on proximity's power, we recognize
its transformative and active place. But as those of us who have
been proximate longer than a brief season know, the relationships we
make through shared history, coupled with the camaraderie and commitment to rebuking oppression, are what sustain us for the long haul.

This change does not come about overnight, but the process makes
us richer. My proximity to the poor did not simply transform me; it
made me a deeper, wider, and stronger person in every way. I did not
realize its power because I sat in a small corner observing from afar
but because I continued to daily push out from the familiar into the
unknown, knowing that the learning curve, while steep, was teaching
me things I needed for my long journey, both personal and collective.

There were times I did not think I was strong enough, but as
anyone who does exercise of any kind knows, you get stronger
along the way.

I have a friend who runs half-marathons. She did not grow up running them, and a few years before she began she was sure she didn't have the ability to run that long or that hard. But one day she decided she would try, and after practicing awhile she found that she had worked up to running ten miles. What seemed insurmountable now seemed closer. If she could run for ten miles then she could run for thirteen-plus.

She shared with me how running these distances, all the while reflecting on the woman those years ago who didn't think she could physically do it, had made her stronger. "You know what, Michelle? I run half-marathons because I am showing myself that I am stronger than I think I am. I think we all are stronger than we think we are."

Whatever the challenges that face us, my takeaway is this: we are stronger than we think we are.

We need to be willing to push ourselves farther than we can imagine, not to wear ourselves out but to flex our small spiritual muscles so they grow big and help us tackle the seemingly insurmountable work God is doing in his world. We join this work because this is what we were created to do!

In proximity to the poor we come to a crossroads, an intersection of God's heart and our agenda. In that space, that stark reality, we must make a choice. Are we going to lean in or are we going to be content with the status quo? Do we believe that something can and will change as a result of our journey?

Not knowing the results of our future sacrifice and labor, we can find ourselves stopping before we even start, confused and afraid at our inability to know what is before us. John Baillie, a Scottish theologian who served the church during two world wars, acknowledges the reality of our desire to have the path made clearer: "I am sure that the bit of the road that most requires to be illuminated is the point where it forks."

Proximity is powerful because it makes us stronger. It enables us to have strength perfected in weakness. In this we allow God's grace to bring us to unimaginable places, for his kingdom and to his credit. Strong people are made because of strong decisions to move forward in weakness.

Becoming Brave

I have heard people refer to me as fearless. This makes me smile because, while I might agree now, it was not my initial story. I was born fearful.

I have a younger sister who was born brave. She never thought twice about trying things. The higher and faster something went, the more likely she was to be in the front of the line waiting to try it. I was nothing like her.

I was a quiet, shy, moody child who was skeptical of unfamiliar things. I was worried I'd get hurt. I would lie awake at night thinking about how I could avoid pain and danger. To this day I have never needed stitches or a cast. I purposely chose a more cautious way to engage life.

As a child I wished I could be free like her and flip all over the place (she was a competitive gymnast), zoom down ski slopes, and follow her in other adventures without fear of potential danger. How did she do it?

But fear won out. Every decision I made then and up until my adult life was carefully measured according to my dread of pain. What started out as avoidance of physical pain morphed into fear of emotional pain, and I worked to keep myself and all that surrounded me safe—safe from broken bones, from hurt feelings, from rejection, from a bad reputation, from friendships that made me look or feel bad. There was no limit to the pains I sought to avoid.

I share this because I want you to know that doing Christian social justice advocacy does not require us to be naturally brave. Sometimes we think people are "wired" for the work they do. And in some ways I have been wired with specific strengths that help me engage serious issues that impact my community, finding solutions to problems and perseverance to finish the job. But being brave was not one of those natural skills.

If you are afraid—and at some level everyone is afraid—you can choose to move past it. I call it choosing courage. Choosing courage is doing the next hard thing in front of you, not worrying about the consequences or what others are doing. It's not looking to the left or the right but walking the path set out for you.

The Next Hard Thing

My life's choices as an adult have taken me on a course of doing the next hard thing in front of me, from my early days teaching in rough schools to walking my children through life as dominant-culture minorities to advocating for politically polarizing issues. My decisions have not been based on how I felt about them; I just chose courage and pushed on in spite of my feelings.

I have always taken great comfort in another young leader in the faith who needed encouragement to choose courage. Timothy was the apostle Paul's young son in the Christian faith. He traveled alongside Paul and even helped write several of Paul's epistles. Even though Timothy was a committed leader in sharing the gospel (in Philippians 2:20 Paul says he has "no one else like him"), he needed help learning to lead in spite of fear. Paul tells him, "For the Spirit God gave us does not make us timid, but gives us power, love and self-discipline" (2 Timothy 1:7). We all need to be reminded that fear is contrary to what God equips us with to accomplish his kingdom work.

It wasn't until May 2009 in Jackson, Mississippi, when I was listening to one of my heroes, Dr. John Perkins, talk about fear and courage, that I was able to articulate the progression of my own personal decisions and journey. Perkins, along with being the founder of the Christian Community Development Association (CCDA), is one of the most memorable and inspirational leaders in the church today—for me and probably everyone else who does what I do.

On my first trip to Jackson and the Perkins Center, I was sitting in a circle of people next to Perkins listening to him talk about fear and courage. As a naturally fearful person I began to scribble as fast as I could to catch his wise words; there was just so much. And then I heard him say something that not only caught my attention but defined the choices of my fear-filled life, especially those affecting my proximate life and my constant battle to lean into the next thing.

"Courage is not the absence of fear," he said. "It is living one's conviction in the face of fear."

Living in proximity to the poor and its pain not only compels us to engage the people impacted but calls us to stand with them on their side, embracing their suffering and their positions.

I was not born into the life of the poor. I was born into an educated family that was on the road to a high level of economic and social success. But I could not engage the pain of the poor from behind the scenes where I could play it safe. I could not do it effectively on the sidelines, fearful of those who would judge me. I would have to do restorative justice work in the center of the road, head held high alongside my brothers and sisters who were suffering. I was not only implicated in their pain; I needed to be proud to stand with them and lift up their cause.

Shaking Knees, Chattering Teeth

Even decades later I still make choices that make my knees shake and my teeth chatter. But I continue to choose courage because I cannot play at two lives. I must be willing to stand on the side of the poor regardless of the cost.

August 2016, prior to Donald Trump's election to the US presidency, was one of those times. The year leading up to that moment had been defined by him insulting immigrants, talking about mass deportation, bragging about building a wall on the Mexico border, and bashing women, people of color, the disabled, and other vulnerable people who lived in my community and in communities all around the world. All the while, seventy percent of white evangelicals were planning to vote for him.

My friends and I have been working a long time on the issue of immigration, and one of my closest friends and allies in this fight has been Noel Castellanos. After Noel walked El Camino de Santiago during his sabbatical, he came back and pitched the idea of doing a camino on behalf of immigration. The details took time to be developed, and somewhere between the sheer exhilaration of organizing such a creative pilgrimage and completing what we said we would do were decisions to ensure that the message of God's heart for the vulnerable and the need for his church to move from awareness to action alongside immigrants would be made publicly.

El Camino del Inmigrante took on a life of its own. It was a beautiful gift to behold as the body of Christ joined the eleven-day, 150-mile journey from the Tijuana–San Diego border to the Metropolitan Detention Center in downtown Los Angeles, pushing into darkness with the light of Christ's gospel, which is resounding good news for immigrants.

At the time, 65 million people all over the world were being forcibly displaced from their homes as a result of conflict or persecution. White evangelical Christians were at a crossroads regarding their vote. Would fear and comfort drive their decisions? Would they allow immigrants and immigration both in our borders and around the world to be part of their decision? Would the Camino message help shape a narrative?

As we came to the final day of our journey, we ended with a public rally at the detention center. Months before I had worked through every detail of where we would be when, what messages we wanted to bring, even who would walk in the front of the line and what I would wear.

If we had done what I hoped, evangelicals around the country would be watching this effort on social media. We would be prophetic and bold, bringing our personally held convictions to a public place at a divisive time. I called my friend and asked him to bring me a Black Lives Matter T-shirt. (Yes, this is the same friend who kindly told me I was allowed to wear one.)

This was something I needed to make public, knowing that others at home in my community were watching. I wanted those in my proximate community to say, "There's Michelle making the statement I knew she would—she's with us." I fought back the fear that those in my former world might say something like, "There's Michelle making the statement I knew she would—she's not with us."

This is a hard thing for me to swallow still, but it is where I am in my life. I love both communities. They are both my family, but the reality is that my family—*our* family—is divided. The body of Christ is divided, and we need healing.

I wore the T-shirt proudly but also a little fearfully. I was mostly scared for our nonprofit back home. Would my choice of clothing leave the poor I love so much without the resources needed to support the church-based nonprofit my husband so courageously and faithfully served?

I remember thinking, *Well, only people who are following us will see. And maybe they won't even notice.* I wasn't ashamed; I was just nervous that we would lose funding—again. I spent that morning pushing back worries, leaning into our message when I finally took the stage: the privileged church that reared me, whose daughter I am, needs to side with the poor. *It is not noble to stay silently on the sidelines. It is time for the church to be the church!*

I left that stage and assembled people in the front to hold our El Camino banner. I put myself smack in the front so white middle-class evangelicals would be represented. I marched with my Black Lives Matter T-shirt on, nearly fainting when I thought about what would become of our nonprofit back home.

We turned the corner to stop and fall to our knees in front of the Los Angeles city building where black clergy and mothers whose sons had been shot by police had taken up residence in order to get a meeting with the local city leaders. At that moment I saw more cameras and reporters than I had ever seen in my life. The flashes directed on my face nearly made me swoon. I was afraid my efforts would ruin everything. I called out in my heart in prayer to God to give me courage to push forward and not be afraid.

At that moment God's Spirit reminded me that our efforts to grow a ministry alongside the poor were not designed to build an earthly kingdom. Our humble work hadn't been undertaken so we could have something to show for our efforts. It had been done so we could stand with the vulnerable before an audience that needed to hear the message from one of their own.

I will never forget that day. It was the end of nearly a year of work. It was physically, mentally, and emotionally exhausting. It was spiritually stretching, developing even seasoned muscles to help me remember that I still need courage to do certain things. I still have a ways to go on my journey toward justice alongside others. And I am stronger than I think I am.

As we listen to and learn about the pain of others, our temptation is to back away or to sit quietly and not engage. To not engage is to miss an opportunity to help people in their pain. We need to go back to the Jericho road. We need to also be willing to fix the road, and to do that we have to face two facts: we will face rejection from those who don't understand our purpose, and we will face failure. We may pour all our energy and efforts into fixing something that stays the same. We will discuss perseverance in the next chapter.

Fear of rejection from those who are content with the status quo or who have the power to keep systems in play is at the very crux of why we need to lean in. Fear keeps leaders from moving forward confidently even when they can clearly see injustice—fear of controversy, rejection, losing followers, being fired. Choosing courage doesn't mean the fear goes away. Choosing courage also doesn't mean we have to be aggressive or abrasive as we work to inspire others to make courageous choices. Jesus himself was filled with grace and truth. Truth is convicting. Truth is powerful. Truth is illuminating. Truth is timeless. Truth sets us free (John 8:32).

The Power of the Collective

For the past several years, pastors and ministry leaders in Colorado have been working to change the dialogue about how people in our state talk about immigrants. Those of us who work and worship alongside immigrants realize that it's not enough for us to know about the pain people experience in the broken immigration system; we need to actually do something with what we know.

Doing something is not an option but rather an opportunity to embrace a new level of leadership.

Issues with a political solution share some basic similarities. They involve a problem in need of fixing, an appropriate solution, and leaders willing to implement the solution even if it means they're criticized. The broken immigration system is a political hot button, so the need for leaders willing to lead regardless of constituent reaction is great.

In my years of experience with organizing, I have regularly called leaders to act on their moral courage when it comes to difficult, polarizing issues. I meet with political leaders who tell me behind closed doors that they know a problem needs fixing but for one reason or another (which is really fear of their constituents) the proposed solution is just not going to work. I meet with pastors who understand what the Bible has to say about injustice but are worried about initiating conversation with their congregations for fear of being too political. Both groups are leaders in their communities; both groups fear those they serve.

Fear is a trap that keeps us in a broken place. When leaders allow fear to keep them from leading, they miss an opportunity not only to help release people from broken systems but to help those they lead to take part in the restoration process.

One summer I worked alongside a group of pastors from Greeley, Colorado, who decided to do a community sermon series on God's heart for the immigrant. They recognized that their congregations needed to look at the issue through a biblical lens and that it was their responsibility to share this message. What these pastors did not realize when they planned to do this was that the national immigration dialogue would unravel about the time the sermon series was to begin. Regardless, they wanted their congregations to receive the message of God's heart for immigrants and to use the

Bible as their guide, not individual political leanings. It turned out to be both a timeless and timely message.

Right before the sermon series was supposed to start, election politics were gearing up and Colorado was one of the most watched states for an election upset. About the time the primaries across the country were ending, with unanticipated and highly reactive results, a story about unaccompanied minors coming across our borders by the thousands broke. Conversations around immigration were politically toxic, not just for politicians but anyone brave enough to engage the dialogue.

This group of pastors leaned in and led their communities as planned. Each week they stood up and boldly spoke up on behalf of God's heart for the immigrant and how we as a Christian community needed to welcome the stranger.

It was a good experience but not without some wear and tear. As anyone in leadership knows, criticism makes leading more about decisive courage than about personal feelings. All of these pastors were put to the test, but their willingness to lead despite fear and congregational reaction gave voice to timeless truth. They generated not only stronger individual convictions but a new momentum for immigrant justice in their congregations. They were and are to be commended.

Fear can tempt leaders to back out. However, when they decide to take courage and do what is right even in the face of fear, our communities are stronger for it.

These pastors were an example of what we hope everyone who sees injustice around them will do—take courage and lead. Their congregations, their communities, and the immigrants in their neighborhoods knew where they stood on God's heart. Church members with differing ideals were called to a more informed view.

One key element of the Greeley story is that it was a collective decision. While even collective decisions can be challenging, at least there is some shared camaraderie. We need support when we have to take courage and lead. We don't have to shoulder this alone. We can find people to lead alongside us and share the journey together.

Running with Redemption in Mind

Once we begin to practice courage, those impacted by injustice see us in a different light. When we move from awareness to action and stand alongside people affected by injustice, they start to trust us in new ways. Vulnerable people are often skeptical of the motivations of outsiders and typically think of our presence as temporary. Maybe we are there because it looks edgy or we want to be viewed in a certain light. Whatever our reasons, they have seen the likes of us before, and when the going gets tough, the temporary get going out of the difficulty and pain.

The more we choose to invest, the more we learn about the pain surrounding an issue and the people it touches. Our presence also becomes a piece of the story. I always wondered where the white church was during the civil rights movement. I hope I would have been in the middle of it, not to make a statement about myself but to help stand with people and make change together.

The longer we stay in something, the more we practice commitment and solidarity with those who are suffering. Yes, we want to change the status quo, but if we don't get what we want—and we probably won't for a while, if ever—at least we get to see just how committed we really are. This practiced perseverance alongside friends who ultimately lose if we all don't win widens our shared experiences and brings us to a place of hopeful journeying.

Remember my friend the half-marathon runner? Imagine the work of engaging injustice as a literal marathon. Imagine the scene of the runners and the crowds. Those who are running are determined to finish the race. They signed up. They have trained. They have committed in a serious way. While there may be varying degrees of participation for the runners, they have all chosen to start and finish the same race. Some do this as a lifestyle; others are trying it for the first time. But all need to decide if they're going to do what they said they will do. Everyone who participates understands that finishing is brutal, and those who don't finish aren't full participants.

What about the onlookers? They are not participants. Don't get me wrong; it's great to run alongside a cheering crowd and it helps build momentum. But the pain of the run—the practicing, the hard work, the decision to finish what you start—is felt only by those who are in the race. Onlookers might have relationships with some of the runners, but they are on the sidelines. They do not experience the shared commitment and pain of finishing the marathon together.

Running a race together is a collective endeavor, one in which we share highs and lows. Regardless of how we finish, when the race is over and we cross that finish line, we are the ones who share in the excitement. We know what we have accomplished, and the celebration is sweet.

After El Camino del Inmigrante and the November election—in which 81 percent of white evangelicals supported a candidate who had spoken disparagingly against immigrants—came and went, the texts, calls, and emails began pouring in. And you know who they were from? My immigrant friends. Immigrant friends, pastors, Dreamers, and mentees who have shared the journey of justice with me were the ones calling.

Together we cried—not because of a presidential candidate or election outcome, as those come and go—but because we were scared of the future. We were grieved that it looked as though the broader, more influential part of the church had not heard our desperation or recognized the injustice. Not all of the notes and calls shared lament and worry; some were words of comfort. Notes read, "I am sorry. How are you? I love you. I am proud of you."

The encouragement came mostly from immigrants who might be directly affected. They were suffering. They were hurting. Although they were the ones the most affected, they reached out to me to see if I was okay. Was it crazy that they would be worried about me? Of course not! We're in this together. They knew we had all worked hard to push against disparaging anti-immigrant rhetoric. They were concerned for my well-being. I was a part of their concern and struggle. I was a part of their pain.

Riding the never-ending highs and lows of our shared journey involves me in the lament of loss and the joy of success. Somehow in the process, someone like me can become a part of the redemption process with the ability to completely rejoice in the celebration. I am a marathon runner in the race too.

Being committed for the long haul comes with those sheer grit moments that demand everyone to ask, "Is it worth it? Will we every stop losing? Will we constantly have to choose courage over fear of rejection, choose hope over skepticism that our efforts have the ability to change injustice?"

Winning and losing are a part of life. When we side with the poor and the vulnerable, somewhere along the way we become poor and vulnerable too. Our life in its best and worst has become so intertwined that we cannot simply walk away. Remember Peter when Jesus asked him if he was going to leave too? "Lord, where are we supposed to go? We know too much to return."

As we stay proximate and choose to deeply engage in the fight for justice, we will have to choose to reengage over and over, building on new strategies, seeking new inspiration to get up and move again. What may have started out as a fearful prospect becomes a way of life. We can't go back, because we have moved from ally to accomplice. We don't want to go back because we believe in what we are doing regardless of fear.

Fear Is So Cliché

When Jesus walked on the earth he healed a man who had been born blind. When those around him asked Jesus about this handicap, they asked what the man's parents had done to cause their son to be born blind. The people of that day were not that much different than those in this day. We want to know who is to blame for our weakness or someone else's. Surely my parents did something wrong so that I was an utterly fearful little girl, right? Nah, they were parents who comforted fears, put me back in bed or back on a bike, and sent me out again. This terrifying fear is something I was born with.

Jesus answered his followers' question with, "Neither this man nor his parents sinned, but this happened so that the works of God might be displayed in him" (John 9:3).

And that is a part of the redemption. If I had stayed in my former world and not moved to a proximate place alongside the poor, I still would have had opportunities to practice overcoming fear because that's a natural part of life and the maturing process. Fear is not unique to a few people but is something that drives humanity.

As we close out this chapter on looking at our fears and moving on despite them, trusting God with the outcome, I would be remiss if I did not mention another naturally fearful leader in our Christian faith—Gideon. Gideon was chosen by God to lead the people of Israel out from under the oppression of the Midianites. The account of his rise to leadership, found in the book of Judges, begins with a visit from the angel of the Lord, who showed up while Gideon was hiding inside a winepress.

Gideon's response to being called a mighty warrior is marked by excuses and worries. But time and time again God comes alongside Gideon, affirming his call and confirming his grace and strength. His first encouragement is "Go in the strength you have . . . am I not sending you?" (Judges 6:14). He then gives the Midianites into the hands of the Israelites despite a 135,000-to-300-man disadvantage. This process enables Gideon to see that it is God who will accomplish what he wants even through a reluctant, fearful person like himself.

When God calls us to practice courage by using our voice, our privilege, our relationships to speak out against oppression, we need to remember the prophet Jeremiah. Jeremiah, referred to as the "weeping prophet" because of his grief and lament for his people, is also afraid to speak truth to those in need of hearing it. God gives him the following "pep talk" to pull himself together and speak truth:

> "Get yourself ready! Stand up and say to them whatever I command you. Do not be terrified by them, or I will terrify you before them. Today I have made you a fortified city, an iron pillar and a bronze wall to stand against the whole land— against the kings of Judah, its officials, its priests and the people of the land. They will fight against you but will not overcome you, for I am with you and will rescue you," declares the LORD. (Jeremiah 1:17-19)

Taking courage and speaking up against injustice not only allows God to use and transform us but enables us to share with those who are suffering, allowing all to be a part of the redemption and transformation process. St. Augustine, one of the most influential leaders of western Christianity, expresses this in an ancient prayer:

> Loving God, who has created humankind in Your own image; grant us grace to fearlessly and boldly contend against injustice, and to make no peace with oppression; and that we may reverently use our freedom, help us to employ it in the maintenance of justice for all people and nations, to the glory of Your Holy Name, through Jesus Christ our Lord. Amen.

My story is the redemption of a woman born fearful who was asked to embrace her fears and reject safety and comfort. After practicing courage over and over again, one day I realized what a fearfully motivated little girl can become—brave. I am brave and delightfully surprised at the transformation.

Choosing to love and embrace those who suffer injustice allowed me not only to share in their process of liberation but to be freed from my own bondage of fear and become brave. I am not that special. Jesus makes us all brave if we take his opportunities to practice courage over fear.

Chapter Eight

SOLVITUR AMBULANDO

At one of my first CCDA conferences, I heard a speaker share the analogy of "going upstream" when you are trying to help hurting people. As a practitioner on the frontlines who sees the results of deep structural injustices, I have witnessed people gasping for air as they are carried down the river. As a young leader who wanted to help, but without the ability to think much past the immediate, I simply grabbed as many bodies as I could and tried to pull them out.

If you pull enough drowning bodies out of the river, you begin to wonder what in the world is happening upstream to throw people in.

I wanted to do what was good and required by the Lord (Micah 6:8). Although difficult, "loving mercy" was a reaction to the present, pressing problems in the immediate moment—pulling people from the river. Taking time to look to a proactive, justice response would require a bit more "doing" and walking upstream. I knew we needed to figure out who or what was throwing our neighbors into the river. Justice requires that we take the time to zoom out from our view of the immediate problem and try to see what got us there in the first place. The more we zoom out, the more we see issues beyond social justice to systemic justice. This requires a different level of active engagement.

Sometimes we don't want to look that deeply because it means we have to walk that much farther upstream. The farther we walk the more layers of the issue we see, and we start to recognize how a person got to this place of needing to be pulled out before they drown. If we want to do effective social justice work, we don't want to wait until half-drowning people get to the bottom but instead pull them out earlier in the process.

Walking alongside single and expectant moms in our community at Open Door clearly pointed to the need for us to begin an early childcare center. When we began, the first preschooler at the center was an energetic little guy the same age as our daughter. They grew up together, at times loyal friends and at others bitter rivals. Such is the nature of childhood relationships. The boy's mom was poor, and in the decades I have known her we have spent many hours watching her work toward various educational opportunities, trying to support her and her son. I met her at church a few years after her son's birth and a nonviolent drug offense that permanently labeled her a felon as an eighteen-year-old.

This family was one of many in our church in similar circumstances, and for this reason we decided to walk farther upstream. We put the preschool program in place to try to fend off generational poverty and suffering. Early intervention is best. We hear that phrase in many scenarios but especially in an educational context. The sooner we can help a child born into poverty gain the skills needed to succeed in school, the better the chance of helping them move beyond their economically binding situation. Combine that with the need for parents to have a place to bring their kids while they work or go to school and to have some Christlike support in training their kids, and you have a great reason to start a preschool.

Our preschool is a great example of doing upstream justice work around individual restoration. There is no substitute for this type of social justice work. But does it get at the bigger issues that caused this child to be born into a family in need of such a high level of support?

I have asked myself this question for years. And it's why I find myself working in faith-rooted organizing and social justice advocacy—to speak into the systemic injustices that keep people and communities in a broken place. As I walked up that river, I realized that the wrongs that needed righting were a lot bigger than I had originally thought, the journey more unfamiliar than I had anticipated.

My sweet friend was labeled with nonviolent felony charges just when her adult life was beginning. For years she worked on educational opportunities that only led her to hear the same thing over and over again—we don't hire felons. No matter how hard she bettered herself through education, the same results ensued: no work for you. Decades have passed and her struggle remains. Her son is now a young man living on his own but his mom still struggles to earn a living wage and keep a place to live.

Now that she no longer has to provide for him, she needs less, but the reality is that her crime committed so long ago never led to her full restoration as a part of society. She could not remove the label, even after she served her time for the original offense. Mandatory minimum sentencing and felony labels kept her permanently struggling, always being swept down the river.

This is not redemptive, nor does it reflect biblical justice. We must strengthen our commitment in our journey toward justice.

It Is Solved by Walking

Choosing to journey the Jericho road as a way of doing justice can feel like we're navigating an unfamiliar road complete with potholes, detours, missed milestones, and overheated engines. We can even find ourselves stranded on the side of the road, wanting to give up and begging for an answer to the question, "Are we there yet?" or, more realistically, "Will we ever be there? How much farther?"

In proximity, our relationships enable us to stay committed for the long haul. We're not fighting for issues; we're fighting alongside the people we love. However, even when we're fighting alongside our family, the timeline of justice work is long, and we can easily become discouraged. We like quick and easy "fixes," but that's not the kind of work we're doing. We're on a long journey that began lifetimes before we arrived and may resolve lifetimes beyond our own.

Proximity is powerful because if we are engaged for a long enough period of time, we inevitably come to realize that ours is not a one-time effort. We cannot offer ourselves once, then sit back and enjoy the fruits of our labor. The work we do and the pain we witness will not end until there is no more injustice. And that is a really long time.

This long-term view of proximity and our chosen place in it can also make us angry, crazy, exhausted, and even cynical because there is often little to show for our efforts. And the efforts we do make are hard to quantify in the context of pragmatic evangelicalism.

So as we move beyond awareness to action, knowing the timeline is long and the results are hard to quantify, how do we move forward? How do we solve the world's injustices? We do it by walking, both figuratively and literally.

Solvitur ambulando is a Latin phrase credited to St. Augustine, which is translated as "It is solved by walking." Augustine lived and taught in the fourth and fifth centuries and was well-acquainted with the culture-challenging dilemmas of his day. He understood not only the practical implications of faith and culture but also delved into the philosophical and ethical issues of the church. Augustine was on a journey toward justice. As fellow kingdom travelers, we also are on a journey in which it can be hard to navigate next steps.

Justice, as you may remember from our discussions in previous chapters, is unlike mercy in that it's not a response to a present felt need but demands that we look beyond the immediate to see how we arrived at this place and how we can correct it the next time. I find it challenging to know next steps. Knowing how to move beyond the immediate and toward effective, sustainable changes can be clear as mud.

Add to all of this personality conflicts, lack of resources, and lack of awareness in those whose help we need and our thinking can become even cloudier. But if we focus simply on putting one foot in front of the other, we can take time to breathe, think, and evaluate where to go next. As we work to persevere in the midst of challenges, we are better able to endure, becoming "mature and complete, not lacking anything" (James 1:4). Regardless of what we see—or rather cannot see—before us, we must "not become weary in doing good, for at the proper time we will reap a harvest if we do not give up" (Galatians 6:9). We need to take time to walk it out, both alone with God and with others.

Walking Together

I find personality tests pretty insightful. It is probably the strategist in me, which happens to be my top characteristic in Strengths-Finder. When I took the StrengthsFinder assessment it did not surprise me that in my top five characteristics was the word "includer." I am about as inclusive as they come. I am just delusional enough to believe that everyone wanting to share the collective journey has a place on the bus somewhere.

Moving toward action packs the proverbial bus as full as possible so that we can drive, walk, and journey together. In order to have a successful ride, we have to listen to and respect (not just tolerate) those who travel with us.

My kids have always attended very progressive schools. In these communities the idea of "tolerance" wasn't just a bumper sticker to be given lip service but a lifestyle to be practiced regularly. This phrase began to bother me as an evangelical from conservative roots. I did not want to practice tolerance or be shown tolerance. "Tolerance" is a fancy word that's really more about putting up with differences than anything else. I don't want people to tolerate my ideas; I want them to respect them.

Respecting people means we sincerely listen to where they're coming from. We value their personhood as well as their contribution. Respect is not waiting for them to be done talking or leave the room so we can sigh with relief—"Whew, that's over!" We need each other. We need to respect each other. We need to listen to each other. We need to hear where others are coming from and be willing to open our minds and learn from them (see Proverbs 27:17).

Tom Tancredo is a former US congressman from Colorado who ran for governor of Colorado some time ago. Tom and I share a few things in common. We are both Italian-Americans living in

Colorado. We are both evangelicals. We both have strong ideas about immigrants and immigration. Yet we are polar opposites in this area.

The summer Tom was running for governor, he was out making friends in new ways and new locations. Governors don't lead a small geographic area where people may think similarly like representatives in the US House do. He needed broad appeal, and while he may have done great legislative work in other areas, the only thing he was known for in my circles was his nationally recognized anti-immigration perspective.

The February prior to the November election Tom was marching in a local MLK parade when he began to engage with my longtime friend and immigration ally Jude DelHierro. Their conversation ended with a request from Jude to meet with me. The call Jude made asking if I'd meet with Tom was not a new suggestion. I had heard it many times.

We started the meeting with a few pleasant exchanges, including how little time we all had available, and Jude opened with prayer. Tom talked about himself a bit and then I asked two questions before I began. For some reason I cannot explain—the Holy Spirit being most likely—I asked if he would meet with me a second time, no cameras or press. Second, I asked, "How does an East Coast Italian from a Catholic family end up an evangelical in Colorado?" His was a journey in which I was keenly interested.

He laughed, knowing the dissonance of his position, and invited me into his story. His family's immigration was the first part and his personal faith narrative was where he wrapped up. We headed out promising to meet for a more lengthy visit at another time.

The second time we met, I took him on a tour of three community ministries that reflected my journey alongside the poor and the immigrant. On the tours we listened to and interacted with people impacted by poverty, immigration, and race.

At the end of meeting number two, we sat in the car a few blocks from my house. I had sensed it still was not time to talk about immigrant justice. We needed another meeting. But we were both so busy, how could either of us find more time? I asked anyway, and to my astonishment he agreed. I remember giving him a little speech before we parted ways.

"Tom, I know we still need to talk about immigration policy and we will get to it next time, but when we do, I don't want you to listen to me like I'm some flaming liberal. I need you to understand that I have come to my thinking through my relationships and my faith and I want you to respect what I have to say."

With tear-filled eyes we looked at each other, and he said something like this: "Michelle, I don't know how, after this day I just spent with you seeing your life and ministry, I could respect someone more. But when we meet I want you to respect me and know that I don't hate people."

It was an emotional moment for both of us. I replied by saying the time we had spent together confirmed not only that he was my brother in Christ but that he was able to hear the voice of the Holy Spirit and follow it.

At our third meeting we talked about immigration policy and theology. Some moments had great clarity and others were pretty hot. At one point I was so frustrated with him that I told him, "Tom, I think God has you in relationship with people like me because you hang around with people who think like you and don't challenge you."

He responded with a chuckle and said, "I agree, but I think that is why God has me in relationship with you too." How right he was!

National narratives against immigrants persist and our need to listen, learn, and work together is ever before us. This is merely one example of working to build bridges between groups with significant differences. Our humanity fears "the other" and erects walls both literal and figurative so we don't have to listen, respect, learn, or potentially change. There is still time for God to finish what he started in those meetings between two evangelical Italians in Colorado with immigration stories of their own. There is still time for shared restorative work.

Walking Still Farther

We are not "there yet" when it comes to injustice until we have packed our bus in such a way that it includes people directly impacted, people who want to help change the status quo, people who share principles around an issue (regardless of faith and political allegiances), people who don't agree but want to try to understand each other and work to compromise, and young people (a group addressed in chap. 9).

The bigger the problem, the more people we need walking together toward the solution. Proximity to injustice enables us to stand alongside people who are directly impacted, but because we come from another place, we can also work to bring coalitions of unlikely groups together.

When we live in proximity to the poor we become used to living, working, and worshiping with people who are different from us. We begin to build bridges based not on our differences but our similarities. Ours is not a natural gathering but rather a chosen element of our shared proximity. It is a choice to believe that regardless of history and hurts, we need each other—especially when we are different.

In the well-resourced community that I came from, the need to show our distinctions was powerful. We all looked relatively similar, lived in similar houses, wore similar clothes, and spoke with similar lingo. But we spent our growing up years distinguishing ourselves from our families and peers. Our conversations were spent highlighting our uniqueness.

This is not the case in my proximate place with the poor. Diversity is very well defined in my community. We already know we're different—our distinctives are obvious—so our tendency is to focus on what we have in common so we can build bridges of unlikely friends and allies. We concentrate on things like having children, wanting to be successful, wanting to love and be loved.

In my work on systemic injustice issues, building coalitions is a must. When you tackle something like homelessness or immigration reform, you need a lot of people. So you create space to bring people who share your ideals together regardless of your foundational group's history. If you share a common problem, you work with anyone who's willing, and that means white evangelicals from the South and African Americans from the ACLU.

When I began to work on immigration reform, it wasn't like I started with the issue itself. My work started with a relationship in my community and the desire to help change a system. At the time I knew no evangelical groups in my city that were actively working to address immigration reform, so I did what any reasonable person would do: I joined the faith groups that *were* working on immigration reform.

I remember my first interfaith immigration meeting. The groups represented included mainline Protestants, Jews, Quakers—it seemed like every faith group I had heard of cared about immigrants except the one from which I hailed: evangelicalism. I sat there a little embarrassed at evangelicals' lack of engagement, seriously offended at our anti-immigrant narrative yet relieved that finally we were going to be represented among people working to help on this important social justice issue.

People were gracious when I told them who I was and where I came from. I thanked them for allowing me to be with them and referred to the story in the Gospels where the pagan woman asks Jesus for mercy for her daughter, knowing she has no right to ask him because he is a rabbi of the Jews. She asks Christ to consider her just like dogs who are allowed to eat the crumbs from the children's table (Matthew 15:21-28). I was happy to simply be a dog, eating crumbs from those who were leading such a noble work.

I knew I didn't deserve a seat at that established table. My faith group had done little to help address the injustice around immigration, and not only that; we had leading evangelical politicians speaking directly against compassion for immigrants. I had some nerve not only sitting at a table of leaders but joining their efforts.

Their model of grace and acceptance is one I will never forget. But it stemmed from their understanding of the need to strengthen coalitions. I needed them to help me engage an issue alongside misinformed people. They needed me to lead my misinformed people. Together we needed to build a faith coalition that included all faiths because immigrants were in all of those groups and needed help. Setting our differences aside, we were going to learn to work together.

Learning to Work Together

There is a lot of fear among evangelicals when it comes to working in interfaith settings. Even if they are willing, they are often concerned about their appearance to other evangelicals. I think we need to focus more on the people's benefit than our own appearances.

The behemoth of immigration reform demands that we look beyond our differences and build bridges based on what we do agree on. This is really what doing justice is all about: building bridges to people who don't think like us. It's about finding what we do have in common and working to grow alongside each other until one day we share the same desires and outcomes and are able to celebrate the same victories. It's a commitment to a set of principles we agree on, respecting the way we both got to this shared space.

Justice work, especially restoration of social and systemic injustice, is about the greater good, not about us or our individuality. If we at the table all believe the road needs restructuring, we need to go with it; our common purpose is the glue that keeps us together. We need each other's strength not to spar but to strengthen our collaborative endeavors. By working alongside people who are different than us, we are able to think bigger and also share resources more effectively, bringing our separate strengths to the collective work.

A terrific example of transformed thinking is seen in the story of Oskar Schindler and Itzhak Stern. This unusual pair worked together during World War II. Schindler was a Nazi and Stern was a Jew. What began as a relationship tied to profit for Schindler became a proximate journey alongside Stern and the Jewish people. This journey changed Schindler into a man who at great financial loss worked tirelessly and creatively to save the lives of twelve hundred Jews.

Recently my younger son read the book *Schindler's List* and together we watched the movie directed by Stephen Spielberg. While this is about the last movie I think a young person should watch, I do appreciate the noble portrayal of Oskar Schindler and was glad my son was inspired by the story. As young people, when we learn about the Holocaust and its atrocities, we find it hard to believe a human being can despise another so much. We are drawn to those stories because in our hearts we want to believe in those who defy the status quo and its ills. We want to believe in the heroes and the people who will call out injustice, not with wishful thinking from behind a closed door, but boldly with direct action.

In this account, Stern creates a list of names of people for Schindler to employ and keep from being sent to their deaths in the gas chambers. At the end of the war Schindler realizes that he will be tried as a Nazi war criminal. But his deep grief is the vast number of people who died and that he could not help enough. After Schindler shares his lament with his Jewish employees, Stern, the accountant and partner who helped him accomplish what he had, reaches out with compassion and comfort. He gives Schindler a ring made from the gold fillings of his employed Jewish workers' teeth. Engraved in it is this phrase from the Talmud: "Whoever saves one life saves the world entire."

Our individual work is a small yet vital effort. Teaming up with friends and unlikely allies is the only way we can move farther upstream to do the deep restructuring work of systemic justice.

People are not our enemies. Injustice is the enemy, as are all the powers that want to keep people in those systems in a broken place. Building bridges to those on the "other side" is how we resist the enemy and his lie that we cannot work together. Why let this lie define and limit us any longer?

I recognize that it's hard to learn to build bridges with those who are radically different from us, even for the best of leaders—on both sides. It's hard to build bridges to an unfamiliar place, especially with all those stereotypes to cross over. I get it. We are naturally closed, skeptical people.

We see this with the prophet Jonah, who is so against bringing good news to his enemies that he runs the other way; he knows God will be compassionate and merciful, and he can't stand it (Jonah 4:1-3). Jonah is so upset that God would extend grace and compassion and unite his enemies under his umbrella of love and concern that when the people repent and turn toward God— joining his table—Jonah wants to die! He would rather perish than build bridges to an enemy.

While we are driving in our bus or walking on the journey, picking up needed friends and allies along the way, we should not be so quick to dismiss their concerns, their voices. We need to stay on the bus together. In my experience I have sometimes been the one driving the bus; I have sometimes been one of the riders, but every time I see people get off, I get sad and feel like we haven't accomplished our mission. I know how much we need each other for this collective journey. We cannot be shortsighted. We need to keep moving up the hill together.

Confident Pluralism

Coalition building is not simply about numbers; it is about personal and collective transformation. Because of the difficult building process, we must ensure that we are building wisely and do not lose people along the way. I often see people hesitate to build bridges toward people who are different because they're not recognizing the value of the strength around what they share.

When I have shared about coalition building in a multifaith environment, I have focused on a shared value—justice for immigrants. The same has been true in building coalitions of conservative and progressive evangelicals. While this is essential work that needs to be done, how do we rationalize working with people who may share a value or two but don't share our other beliefs?

This is where respect and transformation are key. If we are trying to listen, respect, and build bridges, we open ourselves up to the possibility that there is more than one way to do things and our way might not be the best. This is hard to do if we're used to hanging around people who think completely like us.

It's important to recognize that when we work with people of different faiths and politics, we are not watering down our own; we are transforming our perspectives. Think back to Stern and Schindler. Stern did not come to the table fearing that Schindler would turn him into a Nazi and Schindler did not consider that working with Stern would turn him into a Jew. We are not conforming to or adopting each other's identity or faith. We are not watering down what we believe but bringing it to the table alongside others, making the table bigger. If we share a common ground for justice, we should allow that shared space to grow.

Frederick Douglass, a former slave and African American leader in the abolitionist movement, was known for supporting conversations and building bridges to people of different races and ideologies. He suffered criticism from his fellow abolitionists because he was willing to dialogue with slave owners. His famous quote that came of that moment was, "I would unite with anybody to do right and with nobody to do wrong."

This attitude is not typical but it is powerful and essential to making the long walk upstream to move forward. Doing right together is not a minimal effort. It is essential. No single group will ever be able to do the work of justice alone. We need others. We need to be willing to extend hospitality and build a table long enough to invite others to join.

Recently I came across an article written by John Inazu, a law professor at Washington University in St. Louis, calling people in our deeply divided country to embrace what he calls "confident pluralism"—the willingness to draw near to those with different ideologies in order to pursue a common existence. Inazu says we need to recognize our deep differences yet use the freedoms available in our speech to create spaces for better conversations:

> Finding common ground does not mean endorsing every goal or every value of the people to whom we draw near. But it does mean drawing near. That is at the heart of the vision of what I have called "confident pluralism." That vision is a challenge to enter into the reality of pluralism around us to find common ground. And we can do so out of a confidence in our own beliefs.

A long-standing commitment to justice work that includes confronting systems that keep people and often whole segments of our communities in broken places is essential. We know that these injustices cannot be ignored. Even though the walk upstream is longer than we anticipated, harder than we trained for, and filled with a sense of urgency that at times makes us frantic, we will not stop short of the goal: to see God's justice here on earth as it is in heaven.

Long trips are inevitable; weariness among the travelers is nothing new. But our hope is that we will share this journey together so that when one of us asks, "Are we there yet?" we have someone or a whole lot of someones to say, "Not yet, baby; we're walking farther upstream—together."

Chapter Nine

JOINING THE COLLECTIVE ENGAGEMENT

*A*s we come to this final chapter, we need to understand that we are not working toward one great finale this side of heaven. Sure, we are working toward individual victories that are great to achieve, but those of us in proximity to the poor know that for every victory there are numerous other challenges.

A life of proximity to the poor is powerful because its story cannot be wrapped up in one small individual package; it is a collective, faith-filled life lived day after day alongside the pain and suffering of others. We do not simply desire the elimination of pain but a renewed spirit and refined heart as we share it together.

The Old Testament judge Deborah is my hero. It doesn't take much to see why I find her story so inspiring. First, she was a woman leader who had a respected husband in the community

(Judges 4:4)—just like me. She was also a mother (Judges 5:7), so that meant in the midst of her leading she had a bunch of kids around her—also like me. She seemed to be working with a lot of male leaders whom she had to encourage to lead into battle (Judges 4:6-7)—ditto. She wrote music and broke out in song (Judges 5:1), so she was a worship leader and songwriter—again, like me.

Deborah was one of the judges of the Israelites before the establishment of the kings. We learn in Judges 4–5 that she sat under a palm tree helping God's people to make good decisions. Deborah probably did a lot of good during her time, but what she is known for is helping to inspire Barak, the leader of Israel's army, to defeat their oppressors in Canaan. Deborah brought a word from the Lord instructing Barak to fight Sisera's army. Barak, instead of running with it as the army commander, doubted his ability and said he would go only if Deborah went with him.

I often wonder what Deborah was doing when Barak came and asked her to join him in battle. Was she driving kids to school? Folding laundry? Getting a dose of eye-rolling from her teenagers? It's humorous to think that she told Barak to go to war with the Lord's help, and he asked *her* to go with *him*. How she must have been caught between anger and a laugh. Anger that she had to leave what she was doing—dinner, dishes, carpool, school project support—and a laugh that a warrior would need her help when he already had the Lord's.

Regardless, Deborah helps take on Sisera, the leader of Canaan's army. After the battle is over, she breaks out in a celebratory song beginning with this phrase:

> When the princes in Israel take the lead,
> when the people willingly offer themselves—
> praise the LORD! (Judges 5:2)

In addition to all those traits I share with Deborah, I also think she and I have a common passion for unexpected leadership roles (Judges 5:9) and for celebrating success. As a woman leader in her culture, Deborah recognized that she was an unlikely and unexpected part of the circle—another thing I can relate to as a woman leader in an evangelical context.

Everybody expects a king to lead. Everyone wants someone in power to lead them to shared victory. But I have found in the deep work of overcoming injustice that most of the work is accomplished not by the powerful but by the powerless. When young people—our "princes"—lead, when the average person in a community recognizes that something wrong needs righting and willingly takes time to engage what they know, it is time to celebrate and praise the Lord.

A Collaboration of Champions

Becoming proximate to the poor and participating in the powerful, transformational work of alleviating injustice is not an opportunity that's limited to "official" Christian ministry personnel. We should not wait for leaders to invite us to care about injustice or invest in seeing it eradicated. We should not even wait for someone to follow us. As Mother Teresa once said, "Do not wait for leaders; do it alone, person to person."

I don't believe she was talking about working in a silo, and you know I think we should build bridges of coalitions. But I believe she means we shouldn't wait to follow people with big names or big plans before we engage injustice. We do what we need to do on an individual basis. I have found that when we do small work, it grows, because now there is something for others to follow.

There is no doubt that sometimes the "kings of our day" do lead, and when they do, it can be wonderful to watch. But I have also felt the too-frequent sting of leaders who are content to allow a white woman to lead in their stead, cheer in secret, and hope I don't give them a call asking them to join the effort lest their engagement ruin what they have built.

I think that's why we need to include young people in this work. Young people have not built kingdoms to protect or images to maintain. They are working out their hopes and futures and are more often than not willing to work hard—for free—on something that will make the world a better place. They are happy to have their names and efforts stamped all over it and just join in, wherever they're able to support the ride.

What would I have done without all of those wonderful young people who so eagerly listened to the Holy Spirit, found themselves joining the efforts of our shared justice journey, and helped drag me at times to the next thing? Thank you, dear friends. You have made my journey rich and more rewarding.

Young people not only have unmatched energy, they are more computer savvy, social media proficient, and creative! It's a great pairing—seasoned people with work to do and space to highlight it and young people with effort to give and a need to be noticed and affirmed. A collective engagement with youth is something to celebrate, give a shout, and praise the Lord!

The overarching point I'm trying to make is that when we're building a collective effort, it's obvious and easy to go to the "kings" of an institution. Presidents, denominational heads, and megachurch pastors all seem to have the prestige to make big statements on systemic justice issues. We also tend to want a champion for our effort. A champion can help define an issue and represent power and influence.

But I think this is misguided. There is a danger in working with a single leader because it can build walls, not bridges. If we only back one person and their message, we miss the opportunity to shape a grander, more collective narrative. I've seen people want to unite behind one leader in order to belong to something they agree with. I have seen leaders desire to be the solo voice on an issue, and it's hard to watch them jockey for that position.

The reality is that we need a collaboration of champions coming together from across generations, races, cultures, and political side-lines to put their efforts toward injustice. As Christians we need to be united behind one Leader, whose authority, wisdom, and hope for the church transcend time and space. We are followers of our champion—Christ. He calls us to live our lives in service to him and the world in this moment, not to make our name or even our issue great but instead lift high his mission to rescue the world.

Everyone Wants a Hero

Individual justice, societal justice, and systemic justice are all im-portant to God when he looks at restoring creation to its rightful place. People need to be restored along with systems. I believe this is what God intended for his church, with so much history behind us and an unknown future before us. While we need to live with conviction and strong leadership in the moment, we will never make a name for ourselves that outshines what has already been shown.

I am a mother of sons. To be a mother of sons means that for a while—a long while—you know a lot about superheroes. Whether it's Batman-themed birthday parties or Buzz Lightyear costumes, the constant theme of life is superheroes, their superpowers, and their desire to overcome evil with good. I have had more conversa-tions about the color of lightsabers and what that means or what superhero tool is the most awesome than a typical woman needs to have in a lifetime. So goes the journey of motherhood to sons.

I bring this up because this common human narrative—to have someone rescue the perishing and lift up the cause of the victim—pervades our books, movies, and other storylines beyond the world of young boys. Evil must be conquered; good must prevail. I believe that this is a spark of the divine instilled in the heart of all humanity; it is our common denominator in the pain and suffering of the world. We get back up when we are kicked down. We want evil to lose. We work hard to make sure good prevails. We want *justice*. We are desperately hungry and so, so thirsty for *justice* (see Matthew 5:6).

In our humanity we begin to think superheroes will emerge to help us for a time to overcome or right injustice. We may even try to be a superhero ourselves along the way. But I believe this will ultimately burn us out or burn our bridges in destructive ways.

Being proximate to and engaging injustice as a Christian has nothing to do with making a name for yourself. It has nothing to do with being a hero. It has to do with sharing the struggle, following our true hero, and joining the collective narrative that has been written since the beginning of time, when darkness began to push back against the light, bringing pain and injustice to our beautiful world.

A Big Glass of Hope

It was the end of 2014, and protests were taking place all over the country as a result of a series of videos of unarmed black men being fatally shot by the police, yielding no trials for those who shot them. An immigration reform bill—the Border Security, Economic Opportunity, and Immigration Modernization Act passed by the US Senate but not the House—that many of us had poured our energies into passing was set to expire with the new year. The midterm election of 2014 had just taken place with record money spent and record low voter turnout. Our country was skeptical and unengaged. Our minority population was scared and angry. It was a dark time for many, yet it was Advent. This is the point in the spiritual calendar where we celebrate the breaking of the silence so long ago with the coming of Jesus, the promised Messiah.

I was on yet another call with a colleague talking about how we should respond to yet another horrible video of an unarmed black man being killed by the police. It seemed like darkness was snuffing out the glimmer of light. As we sat there in a rare moment of silence he asked me a question that I have been asked more times than I can count during my journey: "How can you continue to work on things that may never change?"

And there it was, the all-too-familiar question dangling, waiting to be answered.

I replied, "I drink a big glass of hope every day when I get up. Some days the glass needed is bigger than others."

Hope is something that stems from the very heart of God and is alive and present in the world. I don't believe it is limited to those who call themselves Christians, but as people of faith, we do have a common shared hope—that God will finish what he started and restore all things to himself, to the perfect peace of shalom.

No more tears, no more pain, no more injustice. Meanwhile we wait in our proximate place in the reality that the day has not yet come. We long for a vision of what can be even if we cannot see it, and we do it by faith.

By-Faith Living

Christians are called to live a life of faith, yet those of us from a privileged place assume that we will see what we hope for. When we are in proximity to the poor, witnessing their alarming pain and stagnation, we think that if we don't see results, we are failing. To make matters worse, even if we're successful on one issue, there are always other issues to engage.

This might cause us to feel deep sadness. But a life lived by faith is deeply hopeful. It is hopeful because we recognize that it's not about us and our efforts. It's not even about the relationships we have with our proximate community impacted by injustice. Something bigger, deeper, and wider is going on.

The author of Hebrews does a great job describing the collective narrative in chapters 11 and 12 of his book. In chapter 11 we see the big names of our faith. Those names have set the stage for Christians throughout history. This chronology of heroes allows us to see how leaning into the pain in the moment can pour into the future faith legacy of those who come after us. With every name and effort recorded in Hebrews 11, we see the insurmountable odds and the unlikely stages that were set, and we realize that we don't have to be superheroes; we just need to follow God's call to live by faith—believing in the result of what we hope for regardless of what we see (Hebrews 11:1).

As Christians who want to do justice, we need to understand our place in the overall picture and adopt a lifestyle of "by-faith living," believing in something we cannot see and being sure it will come to pass. It is this very type of faith-filled living that the "ancients were commended for" (Hebrews 11:2).

And so we see name after name, beginning with the earliest biblical narratives: "By faith Abel . . . By faith Enoch . . . By faith Noah . . . By faith Abraham . . . By faith Isaac . . . By faith Jacob . . . By faith Joseph . . . By faith Moses' parents . . . By faith Moses . . ."

And the list goes on, sharing what each person chose to do in their moment, living by faith, never forgetting to lean into the promise of what was to come, believing until they were no more—

that God would accomplish what he started and restore and redeem brokenness.

As we read through this amazing list of all that was done and who did it, we sense the author grappling with limited space and time to give credit to the people's collective effort. In his haste he drops the actions and just lists the names: Gideon, Barak, Samson, Jephthah, David, Samuel. And from specific names he lumps in what they accomplished and saw—great miracles displaying the power, majesty, and authority of God, who has set justice and righteousness as the foundation of his throne.

The author does not simply end his chorus with echoes of triumph, as though God only showed up to accomplish his work through big names and solid victories. God and his purpose and work are also seen in suffering, when we don't get the final glorious product—and we may even be killed while believing.

Hebrews 11 commends many for giving up their lives, and for being mocked, beaten, imprisoned, and killed. They have left their places of comfort and privilege and followed this vision so that they no longer look the same, act the same, or are able to be the same person they once were. They are wandering around this world, seeing the truth of its sadness but believing in God's redemption and restorative power in such a real way that they keep moving forward, establishing God's kingdom here on earth, like it is in heaven.

They are square pegs in round holes, wandering "in deserts and mountains and in caves and in holes in the ground" (Hebrews 11:38)—or, to bring it into the modern day, hole-in-the-wall places like inner-city churches with chipped paint, broken glass, and thirty-year-old equipment held together with duct tape, small basement nonprofits that no "normal" person trained to teach schoolchildren would be caught dead in, yet where teachers spend countless hours reading to preschoolers.

These are the places along life's Jericho road where we will find ourselves when we follow God's heart for justice. We will not be working in places where the air conditioner blows cool air in the summer or the heater warm air in the winter. We will drive blocks to park our cars and walk to these places, dismal to the commoner's eye, hoping they are still intact when we get there because we know we are working for something that cannot be seen.

We know that those who are beaten up on the side of the road need people who are not beaten up to come alongside them closely, share the journey, and help pave the way for a better tomorrow. Because proximity to injustice is so powerful, we know that these efforts are not merely for our individual justification but instead to build into the collective community's vision. Someday the road will have no more half-dead, beaten-up men, women, or children lying along its side or privileged people with excuses and policies to justify staying unengaged or walking quickly away.

No, there will be a day when our faith will no longer be needed. Our hope no longer a daily choice. The day will come when all we have is love before us, sustaining us, keeping us, restoring us, healing us, because the greatest of these is love (1 Corinthians 13:13). While we wait, we know we must continue to choose hope by faith like those who have gone before us, our great cloud of witnesses (Hebrews 12:1-3).

This great cloud lived by faith up until their deaths. They journeyed until they became strangers to the worlds they had been born into. Knowing they could have returned to their former lives and tried to "fit" back in (Hebrews 11:15), they did not—they pressed on in their pilgrimage in search of a new country. They were on the journey, longing for a vision of the unseen and in search of final restoration. This is why God is not ashamed to be known as their God (Hebrews 11:16). He has prepared a place for them where they can finish journeying and rest.

Further Up and Further In

C. S. Lewis's beloved allegorical tales, The Chronicles of Narnia, speak of journeys of adventure and longing until there is finally rest. In the last book of the series, *The Last Battle*, the final chapter finds us with the main characters walking together and coming upon a pool of water and what look like high, unscaleable cliffs. The falling water, high cliffs, and thundering noise cause them to stop and begin to question their ability to move forward. And then you hear the constant refrain of the journey: "Don't stop! Further up and further in."

As the group continues to push on, they realize that what seemed scary was actually confirming that they should continue further up and further in. Charging forward with confidence, their vision became more clear and they saw Narnia in a different light. Then they entered final peace and rest.

This part of the Narnia tale captures that spot somewhere between love of one's place in the world and the realization that there is life far beyond what we see. As we allow the Spirit to drive us further up and further into his deep transformational work, the journey that seemed so impossible grants sufficient grace and strength to bring us to a place of continued perseverance and joy.

Those listed in the biblical narrative of life lived by faith never saw the fulfillment of the promise: a redeemed world. We are not the same as those Old Testament saints who were waiting for the coming of the Messiah. We have the fullest expression of God's love in his Son Jesus, and he has reconciled us to him and to each other. Yet we are still waiting, hoping, and living by faith that he will come again and rescue us from a world wracked by pain and injustice.

We must continue to fix our eyes on the ultimate seeker and restorer of justice, Jesus, who for the joy and hope set before him endured the cross, died the shameful death of a criminal, and finished what he set out to do (Hebrews 12:2). We follow the one who endured such opposition from sinful men. Do not grow weary and lose heart.

In this collective chorus of those who live by faith, whose eyes are set to a vision of what can be, we can see the bigger picture coming into focus and our role in engaging injustice more clearly. This is not a place of loneliness or cynicism but deep camaraderie. Jim Wallis in his book *God's Politics* says cynicism is a place for those who see what's happening in the world but do not choose to hope. They protect themselves from such a foolish notion that things can change. They remain at a distance from pain and injustice because hope may lead to disappointment.

I have often told people that my choice to hope is not because I see the world through rose-colored glasses. In my proximate place with the poor, bearing witness to injustice, I actually have a very clear picture of what is going on. In that space, my choice to hope is what Wallis describes in his book:

> Hope is a spiritual and even religious choice. Hope is not a feeling; it is a decision. And the decision for hope is based on what you believe at the deepest levels—what your most basic convictions are about the world and what the future holds— all based on your faith. You choose hope, not as a naïve wish, but as a choice, with your eyes wide open to the reality of the world—just like the cynics who have not made the decision for hope.

It is with eyes wide open to the pain, stagnation, brokenness, and oppression in my proximity to the poor that I wake up in the morning and drink my big glass of hope. I recognize my role as a privileged woman implicated in the pain yet surrounded by a great group of people—or, as the author of Hebrews says, "a great cloud of witnesses"—joined in this legacy from life's beginning until now. I have been invited to take part in their collective effort, and now they are bearing witness to my redemptive journey toward justice.

Serenity

When I was a little girl, there was a decoupage plaque outside my bedroom door. During the season that I was learning to read I remember staring at that plaque, working to decipher each word. It was the first thing I learned to read on my own without the help of adults. I would have learned to read it sooner had there not been one unfamiliar and rarely used word. Struggling to sound out each syllable, I assumed that it sounded like "sir-en-ity"—serenity.

It was the most well-known line of the serenity prayer: "God grant me the serenity to accept the things I cannot change, the courage to change the things I can, and the wisdom to know the difference." How beautiful and ironic that this prayer was the first thing I learned to read on my own and has brought me to where I am today.

With all the wrongs that needed righting, I had no idea how insane and angry it would make me to be unable to fix them quickly, easily, or completely. I did not realize how my fear of failure, reputation, and image would have to be overcome to speak out against the status quo and illuminate injustice. Nor did I realize just how much discernment I would need to know what mantles passed on by those who went before me were now mine to wear.

Yes, I would need serenity, lots and lots of serenity. I would also need courage and wisdom.

St. Augustine knew that hope alone would not change our broken world. Hope, not a naive wish but a chosen belief of what can be, does not simply sit in the clouds, keeping us on the sidelines. St. Augustine said, "Hope has two beautiful daughters; their names are Anger and Courage. Anger at the way things are, and Courage to see that they do not remain as they are."

My story is not unique. It has been written for years. But my desire is to share it so that others might be willing to join our efforts. As you consider your awareness of injustice and feel a desire to do more with your privilege, I encourage you to run.

Run further up and further in to the deeply personal and powerful place of proximity, to the brokenness of injustice and oppression in this hurting world. Run with confidence, believing that your sacrificial efforts will bring us all a little closer to the heaven on earth we so desperately long for. Throw off your worries, your fears, your limitations, and join the great cloud of witnesses that have gone before us for thousands of years, and let us run *together* with perseverance the path marked for us.

May God continue to give us the faith to believe he is finishing what he started, a discontent for the status quo of injustice, and courage to ensure that we are actively engaged in our proximity to those impacted by injustice so things no longer remain as they are.

ACKNOWLEDGMENTS

I am deeply grateful to the numerous people who have supported this endeavor both directly and indirectly. Many thanks to Denise Wyn, who helped me gather my thoughts in the earliest stages. Thanks to the IVP team, especially Al Hsu and Helen Lee for helping me learn how to turn thoughts into words on a page in meaningful ways. Thank you to Patty Pell for her affirmation and willingness to help me take the next steps. Special thanks to Daniel Hill, Esperanza Martinez, Louis Carlo, and Christine Nolf for helping reset the stage needed to allow my thoughts to be boldly crafted. Thank you to Don and Patty Wolf for supporting the physical space needed. Thank you Jennifer Isaac for not only clearing space in my calendar but assuring me that if I just took time to sit and write, the content would come.

I am grateful to each person who has lived alongside me, helping me to learn a deeper sense of the power of the gospel and its work in all of us from my earliest years in Dallas to our two-plus decades in Denver. Special thanks to the Open Door community for sharing life together. Special thanks to Ernest and Theresa Mossman for their commitment to us as family. Thank you to Ernesto, Phil, and Jenny—you have been such special mentees-turned-colleagues, giving me a renewed sense of faith in the future church.

Many thanks to Danny Carroll, Jude DelHierro, Luis Villareal, and Jeff Johnsen for your special commitment to seeking justice for immigrants and the flourishing of our city of Denver. You are my band of brothers. I am grateful to my CCDA family but special thanks to Noel and Marianne Castellanos, Lisa Rodriguez Watson, Ava Steaffans, Kit Danley, Amy Williams, Alexia Salvatierra, Miea Walker, Shawn Casselberry, Matthew Soerens, Dominique Gilliard, Leroy Barber, Wendy Tarr, Ian Danley, Barbara Williams-Skinner, Mary Nelson, Troy Jackson, and Marshall Hatch for so many shared years of support and inspiration.

I am grateful to my family and especially my parents Dennis and Chris for their commitment to serve the church and for always ensuring that we understood that life without Christ was not living. To my three amazing kids—Sydney, Alec, and William—who have shared their parent's journey in the sincerest ways. You have been some of my greatest teachers. I could not be more proud of the people you are growing into. To David, thank you is much too simplistic. You are my greatest cheerleader. Thank you for each silent prayer and every encouraging word to move forward into the calling God has placed on my life. Thank you for your courage to continually push against the grain of groupthink, beyond the familiar to what we know as our life. The journey has been so very sweet.

NOTES

2 Deeper and Higher

29 *Just Generosity*: Ron Sider, *Just Generosity: A New Vision for Overcoming Poverty in America* (Grand Rapids: Baker, 1999), 61.

40 *Dreamers*: The DREAM Act, or Development, Relief and Education for Alien Minors Act, was a never-passed bill that would have granted legal status to undocumented immigrants brought to the United States as children who went to school here.

41 *A true revolution*: Martin Luther King Jr., "Beyond Vietnam," April 4, 1967, New York. http://kingencyclopedia.stanford.edu/encyclopedia /documentsentry/doc_beyond_vietnam.

3 Embracing Brokenness

50 *One learns of*: Chaim Potok, *The Chosen* (New York: Random House, 1967), 265.

52 *A minister is not*: Henri Nouwen, *The Wounded Healer* (New York: Doubleday, 1972), 92.

53 *community and how it is birthed*: Ibid., 94.

    we must be willing: Ibid., 99.

    He says this requires: Ibid., 100.

    It is exactly: Ibid.

54 *For the first time*: Bryan Stevenson, *Just Mercy* (New York: Speigel and Grau, 2015), 288.

    We can embrace: Ibid., 289.

59 *drug scheduling*: "Drug Schedules," United States Drug Enforcement Administration, US Department of Justice, www.dea.gov/druginfo /ds.shtml.

62   *The term justice*: Soong-Chan Rah, *Prophetic Lament: A Call for Justice in Troubled Times* (Downers Grove, IL: InterVarsity Press 2015), 147.

4 Leaning into Love

80   *I have learned*: Andy Cannon, personal interaction with author.

81   *Through Jesus*: Robert E. Webber, *The Younger Evangelicals* (Grand Rapids: Baker, 2002), 242.

82   *The world*: G. K. Chesterton, *Orthodoxy* (Chicago: Moody Bible Institute, 2009), 102.

83   *We weren't created for*: Jeanne Damoff, "In a World of Increasing Terrorism, What Is the Biggest Threat to the Church?," Ann Voskamp (blog), January 7, 2016, www.aholyexperience.com/2016/01/in-a-world -of-increasing-terrorism-what-is-the-biggest-threat-to-the-church.

85   *How do you pick up*: *The Lord of the Rings: The Return of the King*, directed by Peter Jackson (2003; WingNut Films/The Saul Zaentz Company).

5 Race Matters

88   *They don't know many*: The Public Religion Research Institute's 2013 American Values Survey found that the social networks of white Americans are 91 percent white, with 75 percent of whites having entirely white social networks. Daniel Cox, Juhem Navarro-Rivera, and Robert Jones, "In Search of Libertarians in America," PRRI, October 29, 2013, www.prri.org/research/2013-american-values-survey.

89   *Helms categorizes*: Janet E. Helms, *A Race Is a Nice Thing to Have: A Guide to Being a White Person or Understanding the White Persons in Your Life* (Topeka, KS: Content Communications, 1992).

104   *Show me the suffering*: Cesar Chavez, "Prayer of the Farm Workers' Struggle," United Farm Workers, www.ufw.org/_board .php?mode=view&b_code=cc_his_research&b_no=9994.

6 Privilege Needs to Take a Side

115   *Lawrence Kohlberg's stages of moral development*: Lawrence Kohlberg, *The Philosophy of Moral Development* (New York: Harper & Row, 1981).

122   *Letter from a Birmingham Jail*: Martin Luther King Jr., "Letter from a Birmingham Jail," African Studies Center, University of Pennsylvania,

April 16, 1963, www.africa.upenn.edu/Articles_Gen/Letter_Birming
ham.html.

123   *Shallow understanding*: Ibid.

       will have to repent: Ibid.

       Night: Elie Wiesel, *Night* (New York: Bantam, 1982).

124   *If I survived*: Michiko Kakutani, "Wiesel: No Answers, Only Ques-
       tions," *New York Times*, April 7, 1981, www.nytimes.com/1981/04/07
       /books/wiesel-no-answers-only-questions.html.

125   *Neutrality helps the oppressor*: Elie Wiesel, "Elie Wiesel—Acceptance
       Speech," Nobelprize.org, December 10, 1986, www.nobelprize.org
       /nobel_prizes/peace/laureates/1986/wiesel-acceptance_en.html.

7 Fear, Courage, Redemption

130   *I am sure that*: John Baillie, *Invitation to Pilgrimage* (New York:
       Scribners, 1942), 8.

135   *65 million*: Adrian Edwards, "Global Forced Displacement Hits
       Record High," UNHCR, The UN Refugee Agency, June 20, 2016,
       www.unhcr.org/en-us/news/latest/2016/6/5763b65a4/global-forced
       -displacement-hits-record-high.html.

145   *Loving God*: Augustine, "Litany for Social Justice," Prayerful Anglican
       (blog), September 1, 2013, prayerfulanglican.wordpress.com/2013/09
       /01/litany-for-social-justice.

8 Solvitur Ambulando

151   *StrengthsFinder*: Tom Rath, *StrengthsFinder 2.0* (New York: Gallup
       Press, 2007).

157   *Schindler's List*: Thomas Keneally, *Schindler's List* (New York: Scribner,
       1982).

161   *Finding common ground*: John Inazu, "Do Black Lives Matter to Evan-
       gelicals?," *Washington Post*, January 6, 2016, www.washingtonpost.com
       /news/acts-of-faith/wp/2016/01/05/do-black-lives-matter-to
       -evangelicals.

9 *Joining the Collective Engagement*

172 *Don't stop!*: C. S. Lewis, *The Last Battle*, The Chronicles of Narnia (New York: HarperCollins, 2002), 217-28.

173 *God's Politics*: Jim Wallis, *God's Politics: Why the Right Gets It Wrong and the Left Doesn't Get It* (New York: HarperOne, 2005).

Hope is a spiritual: Ibid., 347.

C|C CHRISTIAN COMMUNITY
D|A DEVELOPMENT ASSOCIATION

The Christian Community Development Association (CCDA) is a network of Christians committed to engaging with people and communities in the process of transformation. For over twenty-five years, CCDA has aimed to inspire, train, and connect Christians who seek to bear witness to the Kingdom of God by reclaiming and restoring under-resourced communities. CCDA walks alongside local practitioners and partners as they live out Christian Community Development (CCD) by loving their neighbors.

CCDA was founded in 1989 under the leadership of Dr. John Perkins and several other key leaders who are engaged in the work of Christian Community Development still today. Since then, practitioners and partners engaged in the work of the Kingdom have taken ownership of the movement. Our diverse membership and the breadth of the CCDA family are integral to realizing the vision of restored communities.

The CCDA National Conference was birthed as an annual opportunity for practitioners and partners engaged in CCD to gather, sharing best practices, seeking encouragement, inspiration, and connection to other like-minded Christ-followers, committed to ministry in difficult places. For four days, the CCDA family, coming from across the country and around the world, is reunited around a common vision and heart.

Additionally, the CCDA Institute serves as the educational and training arm of the association, offering workshops and trainings in the philosophy of CCD. We have created a space for diverse groups of leaders to be steeped in the heart of CCD and forge lifelong friendships over the course of two years through CCDA's Leadership Cohort.

CCDA has a long-standing commitment to the confrontation of injustice. Our advocacy and organizing is rooted in Jesus' compassion and commitment to Kingdom justice. While we recognize there are many injustices to be fought, as an association we are strategically working on issues of immigration, mass incarceration, and education reform.

To learn more, visit www.ccda.org/ivp.

TITLES FROM CCDA

Embrace
978-0-8308-4471-5

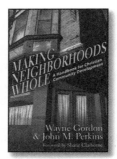

**Making
Neighborhoods Whole**
978-0-8308-3756-4

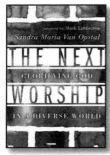

The Next Worship
978-0-8308-4129-5

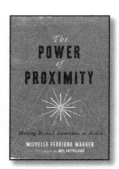

**The Power of
Proximity**
978-0-8308-4390-9

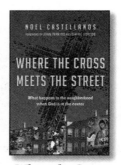

**Where the Cross
Meets the Street**
978-0-8308-3691-8

White Awake
978-0-8308-4393-0

www.ivpress.com/ccda